BEYOND THERAPY

BEYOND THERAPY

Christopher Durang

Nelson Doubleday, Inc.
Garden City, New York

BEYOND THERAPY was first presented by the Phoenix Theatre in New York City on January 1, 1981. The production was directed by Jerry Zaks; scenery by Karen Schultz; costumes by Jennifer von Mayrhauser; lighting by Richard Nelson; sound by David Rapkin. The cast was as follows:

PRUDENCE	*Sigourney Weaver*
BRUCE	*Stephen Collins*
DR. STUART FRAMINGHAM	*Jim Borelli*
MRS. CHARLOTTE WALLACE	*Kate McGregor-Stewart*
BOB	*Jack Gilpin*
ANDREW	*Conan McCarty*
PAUL*	*Nick Stannard*

* The character of Paul, a former suitor of Prudence's, appeared in the final scene of the play at the Phoenix. This character has been written out for future productions, and thus does not appear in this edition.

BEYOND THERAPY

THE CHARACTERS

PRUDENCE
BRUCE
DR. STUART FRAMINGHAM, psychiatrist
MRS. CHARLOTTE WALLACE, psychologist
BOB
ANDREW

ACT ONE

ACT I

Scene 1

(*A restaurant. Bruce is seated, looking at his watch. He is 30–34, fairly pleasant looking, probably wearing a blazer. Enter Prudence, 29–32, attractive, semi-dressed up in a dress or nice skirt and blouse. After hesitating a moment, she crosses to Bruce*)

PRUDENCE: Hello.

BRUCE: Hello.

PRUDENCE: (*Perhaps referring to a newspaper in her hand—The New York Review of Books?*) Are you the white male, 30 to 35, 6'1", blue eyes, who's into rock music, movies, jogging and quiet evenings at home?

BRUCE: Yes, I am.
(*Stands*)

PRUDENCE: Hi, I'm Prudence.

BRUCE: I'm Bruce.

3

PRUDENCE: Nice to meet you.

BRUCE: Won't you sit down?

PRUDENCE: Thank you. (*Sits*) As I said in my letter, I've never answered one of these ads before.

BRUCE: Me neither. I mean, I haven't put one in before.

PRUDENCE: But this time I figured, why not?

BRUCE: Right. Me too. (*Pause*) I hope I'm not too macho for you.

PRUDENCE: No. So far you seem wonderful.

BRUCE: You have lovely breasts. That's the first thing I notice in a woman.

PRUDENCE: Thank you.

BRUCE: You have beautiful contact lenses.

PRUDENCE: Thank you. I like the timbre of your voice. Soft but firm.

BRUCE: Thanks. I like *your* voice.

PRUDENCE: Thank you. I love the smell of Brut you're wearing.

BRUCE: Thank you. My male lover Bob gave it to me.

PRUDENCE: What?

BRUCE: You remind me of him in a certain light.

PRUDENCE: What?

BRUCE: I swing both ways actually. Do you?

PRUDENCE: I don't know. I always insist on the lights being out.
(*Pause*)

BRUCE: I'm afraid I've upset you now.

PRUDENCE: No, it's nothing really. It's just that I hate gay people.

BRUCE: I'm not gay. I'm bisexual. There's a difference.

PRUDENCE: I don't really know any bisexuals.

BRUCE: Children are all innately bisexual, you know. If you brought a child to Plato's Retreat, he'd be attracted to both sexes.

PRUDENCE: I should imagine he'd be terrified.

BRUCE: Well, he might be, of course. I've never taken a child to Plato's Retreat.

PRUDENCE: I don't think they let you.

BRUCE: I don't really know any children. (*Pause*) You have wonderful eyes. They're so deep.

PRUDENCE: Thank you.

BRUCE: I feel like I want to take care of you.

PRUDENCE: (*Liking this tact better*) I would like that. My favorite song is "Someone to Watch Over Me."

BRUCE: (*Sings softly*) "There's a somebody I'm longing duh duh . . ."

5

PRUDENCE: Yes. Thank you.

BRUCE: In some ways you're like a little girl. And in some ways you're like a woman.

PRUDENCE: How am I like a woman?

BRUCE: (*Searching, romantically*) You . . . dress like a woman. You wear eye shadow like a woman.

PRUDENCE: You're like a man. You're tall, you have to shave. I feel you could protect me.

BRUCE: I'm deeply emotional. I like to cry.

PRUDENCE: Oh I wouldn't like that.

BRUCE: But I *like* to cry.

PRUDENCE: I don't think men should cry unless something falls on them.

BRUCE: That's a kind of sexism. Men have been programmed not to show feeling.

PRUDENCE: Don't talk to me about sexism. You're the one who talked about my breasts the minute I sat down.

BRUCE: I feel like I'm going to cry now.

PRUDENCE: Why do you want to cry?

BRUCE: I feel you don't like me enough. I think you're making eyes at the waiter.

PRUDENCE: I haven't even seen the waiter.
(Bruce *cries*)

6

PRUDENCE: *Please,* people are staring at us. They'll think it's something I said.

BRUCE: (*Stops crying after a bit*) I feel better after that. You have a lovely mouth.

PRUDENCE: Thank you.

BRUCE: I can tell you're very sensitive. I want you to have my children.

PRUDENCE: Thank you.

BRUCE: Do you feel ready to make a commitment?

PRUDENCE: I feel I need to get to know you better.

BRUCE: I feel we agree on all the issues. I feel that you like rock music, movies, jogging, and quiet evenings at home. I think you hate shallowness. I bet you never read *People* magazine.

PRUDENCE: I do read it. I write for it.

BRUCE: I write for it too. Free lance actually. I send in letters. They printed one of them.

PRUDENCE: Oh, what was it about?

BRUCE: I wanted to see Gary Gilmore executed on television.

PRUDENCE: Oh yes, I remember that one.

BRUCE: Did you identify with Jill Clayburgh in "An Unmarried Woman"?

PRUDENCE: Uh, yes, I did.

7

BRUCE: Me too. We agree on everything. I want to cry again.

PRUDENCE: I don't like men to cry. I want them to be strong.

BRUCE: You'd quite like Bob then.

PRUDENCE: Who?

BRUCE: You know.

PRUDENCE: Oh.

BRUCE: I feel I'm irritating you.

PRUDENCE: No. It's just that it's hard to get to know someone. And the waiter never comes, and I'd like to order.

BRUCE: Let's start all over again. Hello. My name is Bruce.

PRUDENCE: Hello.

BRUCE: Prudence. That's a lovely name.

PRUDENCE: Thank you.

BRUCE: That's a lovely dress.

PRUDENCE: Thank you. I like your necklace. It goes nicely with your chest hair.

BRUCE: Thank you. I like your nail polish.

PRUDENCE: I have it on my toes too.

BRUCE: Let me see.
(She *puts bare foot on the table*)

BRUCE: I think it's wonderful you feel free enough with me to put your feet on the table.

PRUDENCE: I didn't put my feet on the table. I put one foot. I was hoping it might get the waiter's attention.

BRUCE: We agree on everything. It's amazing. I'm going to cry again. (*Weeps*)

PRUDENCE: *Please*, you're annoying me.
(He *continues to cry*)

PRUDENCE: What is the matter?

BRUCE: I feel you're too dependent. I feel you want me to put up the storm windows. I feel you should do that.

PRUDENCE: I didn't say anything about storm windows.

BRUCE: You're right. I'm wrong. We agree.

PRUDENCE: What kind of childhood did you have?

BRUCE: Nuns. I was taught by nuns. They really ruined me. I don't believe in God anymore. I believe in bran cereal. It helps prevent rectal cancer.

PRUDENCE: Yes, I like bran cereal.

BRUCE: I want to marry you. I feel ready in my life to make a long-term commitment. We'll live in Connecticut. We'll have two cars. Bob will live over the garage. Everything will be wonderful.

PRUDENCE: I don't feel ready to make a long-term commitment to you. I think you're insane. I'm going to go now.

BRUCE: Please don't go.

PRUDENCE: I don't think I should stay.

BRUCE: Don't go. They have a salad bar here.

PRUDENCE: Well, maybe for a little longer.
(She *sits down again*)

BRUCE: You're afraid of life, aren't you?

PRUDENCE: Well . . .

BRUCE: Your instinct is to run away. You're afraid of feeling, of emotion. That's wrong, Prudence, because then you have no passion. Did you see *Equus?* That doctor felt it was better to blind eight horses in a stable with a metal spike than to have no passion. (*Holds his fork*) In my life I'm not going to be afraid to blind the horses, Prudence.

PRUDENCE: You ought to become a veterinarian.

BRUCE: (*Very offended*) You've missed the metaphor.

PRUDENCE: I haven't missed the metaphor. I made a joke.

BRUCE: You just totally missed the metaphor. I could never love someone who missed the metaphor.

PRUDENCE: Someone should have you committed.

BRUCE: I'm not the one afraid of commitment. You are.

PRUDENCE: Oh, dry up.

BRUCE: I was going to give you a fine dinner and then take you to see *The Tree of Wooden Clogs* and then home to my place for sexual intercourse, but now I think you should leave.

PRUDENCE: You're not rejecting me, buddy. I'm rejecting you. You're a real first-class idiot.

BRUCE: And you're a castrating, frigid bitch!
(She *throws a glass of water in his face;* he *throws water back in her face.* They *sit there for a moment, spent of anger, wet*)

PRUDENCE: Absolutely nothing seems to get that waiter's attention, does it?
(Bruce *shakes his head "no."* They *sit there, sadly*)

ACT I

Scene 2

Psychologist's office. Dr. Stuart Framingham. *Very masculine, a bit of a bully, wears boots, jeans, a tweed sports jacket, open sports shirt. Maybe has a beard.*

STUART: (*Speaking into intercom*) You can send the next patient in now, Betty.
(*Enter* Prudence. She *sits*)

STUART: (*After a moment*) So, what's on your mind this week?

PRUDENCE: Oh I don't know. I had that Catherine the Great dream again.

STUART: Yeah?

PRUDENCE: Oh I don't know. Maybe it isn't Catherine the Great. It's really more like National Velvet.

STUART: What do you associate to National Velvet?

PRUDENCE: Oh I don't know. Childhood.

STUART: Yes?

PRUDENCE: I guess I miss childhood where one could look to a horse for emotional satisfaction rather than a person. I mean, a horse never disappointed me.

STUART: You feel disappointed in people?

PRUDENCE: Well every man I try to have a relationship with turns out to be crazy. And the ones that aren't crazy are dull. But maybe it's me. Maybe I'm really looking for faults just so I won't ever have a successful relationship. Like Michael last year. Maybe he was just fine, and I made up faults that he didn't have. Maybe I do it to myself. What do you think?

STUART: What I think doesn't matter. What do you think?

PRUDENCE: But what do *you* think?

STUART: It's not my place to say.

PRUDENCE: (*Irritated*) Oh never mind. I don't want to talk about it.

STUART: I see. (*Makes a note*)

PRUDENCE: (*Noticing* he's *making notes; to make up*) I did answer one of those ads.

STUART: Oh?

PRUDENCE: Yes.

STUART: How did it work out?

PRUDENCE: Very badly. The guy was a jerk. He talked about my breasts, he has a male lover, and he wept at the table. It was really ridiculous. I should have known better.

STUART: Well, you can always come back to me, babe. I'll light your fire for you anytime.

PRUDENCE: Stuart, I've told you, you can't talk to me that way if I'm to stay in therapy with you.

STUART: You're mighty attractive when you're angry.

PRUDENCE: Stuart . . . Dr. Framingham, many women who have been seduced by their psychiatrists take them to court . . .

STUART: Yeah, but you wanted it, baby . . .

PRUDENCE: How could I have "wanted" it? One of our topics has been that I don't know what I want.

STUART: Yeah, but you wanted that, baby.

PRUDENCE: Stop calling me baby. Really, I must be out of my mind to keep seeing you. Obviously you can't be my therapist after we've had an affair.

STUART: Two lousy nights aren't an affair.

PRUDENCE: You never said they were lousy.

STUART: They were great. You were great. I was great. Wasn't I, baby? It was the fact that it was only two nights that was lousy.

PRUDENCE: Dr. Framingham, it's the common belief that it is wrong for therapists and their patients to have sex together.

STUART: Not in California.

PRUDENCE: We are not in California.

STUART: We could move there. Buy a house, get a jacuzzi.

PRUDENCE: Stuart . . . Dr. Framingham, we're not right for one another. I feel you have masculinity problems. I hate your belt buckle. I didn't really even like you in bed.

STUART: I'm great in bed.

PRUDENCE: (*With some hesitation*) You have problems with premature ejaculation.

STUART: Listen, honey, there's nothing premature about it. Our society is paced quickly, we all have a lot of things to do. I ejaculate quickly on purpose.

PRUDENCE: I don't believe you.

STUART: Fuck you, cunt.

PRUDENCE: (*Stands*) Obviously I need to find a new therapist.

STUART: Okay, okay. I lost my temper. I'm sorry. But I'm human. Prudence, that's what you have to learn. People *are* human. You keep looking for perfection. You need to learn to accept imperfection. I can help you with that.

PRUDENCE: Maybe I really should sue you. I mean, I don't think you should have a license.

STUART: Prudence, you're avoiding the issue. The issue is you, not me. You're unhappy, you can't find a relationship you like, you don't like your job, you don't like the world. You *need* my help. I mean, don't get hung up on who should have a license. The issue is I can help you fit into the world. (*Very sincerely, sensitively*) Really I can. Don't run away.

PRUDENCE: (*Sits*) I don't think I believe you.

STUART: That's okay. We can work on that.

PRUDENCE: I don't know. I really don't think you're a good therapist. But the others are probably worse, I'm afraid.

STUART: They are. They're much worse. Really I'm very nice. I *like* women. Most men don't.

PRUDENCE: I'm getting one of my headaches again. (*Holds her forehead*)

STUART: Do you want me to massage your neck?

PRUDENCE: Please don't touch me.

STUART: Okay, okay. (*Pause*) Any other dreams?

PRUDENCE: No.

STUART: Perhaps we should analyze why you didn't like the man you met through the personal ad.

PRUDENCE: I . . . I . . . don't want to talk anymore today. I want to go home.

STUART: You can never go home again.

PRUDENCE: Perhaps not. But I can return to my apartment. You're making my headache worse.

STUART: I think we should finish the session. I think it's important.

PRUDENCE: I just can't talk anymore.

STUART: We don't have to talk. But we have to stay in the room.

PRUDENCE: How much longer?

STUART: (*Looks at watch*) Thirty minutes.

PRUDENCE: All right. But I'm not going to talk anymore.

STUART: Okay.
(*Pause; they* stare at one another)

STUART: You're very beautiful when you're upset.

PRUDENCE: Please don't you talk either.
(They *stare at each other; lights dim*)

ACT I
Scene 3

The office of Charlotte Wallace. *Probably reddish hair, bright clothing; a Snoopy dog on her desk. If there are walls in the set around her, they have drawings done by children.*

CHARLOTTE: (*Into intercom*) You may send the next patient in, Marcia. (She *arranges herself at her desk, smiles in anticipation. Enter* Bruce. He *sits*) Hello.

BRUCE: Hello. (*Pause*) Should I just begin?

CHARLOTTE: Would you like to begin?

BRUCE: I threw a glass of water at someone in a restaurant.

CHARLOTTE: Did you?

BRUCE: Yes.

CHARLOTTE: Did they get all wet?

BRUCE: Yes.
(*Silence*)

CHARLOTTE: Did I show you this drawing?

BRUCE: I don't remember. They all look alike.

CHARLOTTE: It was drawn by an emotionally disturbed three-year-old. His parents beat him every morning after breakfast. Orange juice, Toast, Special K.

BRUCE: Uh-huh.

CHARLOTTE: Do you see the point I'm making?

BRUCE: Yes, I do, sort of. (*Pause*) What point are you making?

CHARLOTTE: The point is that when a porpoise first comes to me, it is often immediately clear . . . Did I say porpoise? What word do I want? Porpoise. Pompous. Pom Pom. Paparazzi. Polyester. Pollywog. Olley olley oxen free. Patient. I'm sorry, I mean patient. Now what was I saying?

BRUCE: Something about when a patient comes to you.

CHARLOTTE: Give me more of a clue.

BRUCE: Something about the child's drawing and when a patient comes to you?

CHARLOTTE: Yes. No, I need more. Give me more of a hint.

BRUCE: I don't know.

CHARLOTTE: Oh I hate this, when I forget what I'm saying. Oh, damn. Oh, damn damn damn. Well, we'll just have to forge on. You say something for a while, and I'll keep trying to remember what I was saying. (She *puts her hands over her eyes and moves her lips*)

BRUCE: (*After a bit*) Do you want me to talk?

CHARLOTTE: Would you like to talk?

BRUCE: I had an answer to the ad I put in.

CHARLOTTE: Ad?

BRUCE: Personal ad.

CHARLOTTE: (*Remembering, happy*) Oh, yes. Personal ad. I told you that was how the first Mr. Wallace and I met. Oh yes. I love personal ads. They're so basic. Did it work out for you?

BRUCE: Well, I liked her, and I tried to be emotionally open with her. I even let myself cry.

CHARLOTTE: Good for you!

BRUCE: But she didn't like me. And then she threw water in my face.

CHARLOTTE: Oh, dear. I'm so sorry. One has to be so brave to be emotionally open and vulnerable. Oh, you poor thing. I'm going to give you a hug. (She *hugs him*) What did you do when she threw water in your face?

BRUCE: I threw it back in her face.

CHARLOTTE: Oh good for you! Bravo! (She *barks for Snoopy and bounces him up and down*) Ruff ruff ruff! Oh, I feel you getting so much more emotionally expressive since you've been in therapy. I'm proud of you.

BRUCE: Maybe it was my fault. I probably came on too strong.

CHARLOTTE: Life is so difficult. I know when I met the second Mr. Wallace . . . you know, it's so strange, all my husbands have had the same surname of Wallace, this has been a theme in my own analysis . . . Well, when I met the second Mr. Wallace, I got a filing cabinet caught in my throat . . . I don't mean a filing cabinet. What do I mean? Filing cabinet, frying pan, frog's eggs, faculty wives, frankincense, fornication, follies bregère, falling falling, fork, fish fork, fish bone. I got a fish bone caught in my throat.
(*Smiles. Long silence*)

BRUCE: And did you get it out?

CHARLOTTE: Oh yes. Then we got married, and we had quite a wonderful relationship for a while, but then he started to see this fish wife and we broke up. I don't mean fish wife, I mean waitress. Is that a word, waitress?

BRUCE: Yes. Woman who works in a restaurant.

CHARLOTTE: No, she didn't work in a restaurant, she worked in a department store. Sales . . . lady. That's what she was.

BRUCE: That's too bad.

CHARLOTTE: He was buying a gift for me, and then he ran off with the saleslady. He never even gave me the gift, he just left me a note. And then I was so very alone for a while. (*Cries. Stops crying*) I'm afraid I'm taking up too much of your session. I'll knock a few dollars off the bill. You talk for a while. I'm getting tired anyway.

BRUCE: Well, so I'm sort of afraid to put another ad in the paper since seeing how this one worked out.

CHARLOTTE: Oh, don't be afraid! Never be afraid to risk, to risk! I've told you about *Equus*, haven't I? That doctor, Doctor Dysart, with whom I greatly identify, saw that it was better to risk madness and to blind horses with a metal spike, than to be safe and conventional and dull. Ecc, ecc, equus! Naaaaaaay! (*For Snoopy*) Ruff ruff ruff!

BRUCE: So you think I should put in another ad?

CHARLOTTE: Yes I do.

BRUCE: I'd be embarrassed to put in the same one again. I mean people who read it will know things didn't work out if they see it again.

CHARLOTTE: Well we'll just make up a new one. What was your first one?

BRUCE: White male, 30 to 35, 6'1", blue eyes, into rock music, movies, jogging and quiet evenings at home, seeks attractive woman for serious relationship.

CHARLOTTE: Well that's good, but not special enough. You need an ad that will get someone more exceptional, someone who can appreciate your uniqueness.

BRUCE: (*Sort of pleased*) In what ways am I unique?

CHARLOTTE: Oh I don't know, the usual ways. Now let's see. (*Writing on pad*) White male, 30 to 35, 6'1", no—6'4", green eyes, Pulitzer Prize winning author, into Kierkegaard, Mahler, Joan Didion and sex, seeks similar-minded attractive female for unique encounters. Sense of humor a must. Write box whatever whatever. There, that should catch you someone excellent. Why don't you take this out to the office, and my dirigible will type it for you. I don't mean dirigible, I mean Saskatchewan.

BRUCE: Secretary.

CHARLOTTE: Yes, that's what I mean.

BRUCE: You know we haven't mentioned how my putting these ads in the paper for women is making Bob feel. He's real hostile about it.

CHARLOTTE: Who's Bob?

BRUCE: He's the guy I've been living with for a year.

CHARLOTTE: Bob. Oh dear. I'm sorry. I thought you were someone else for this whole session. You're not Thomas Norton?

BRUCE: No, I'm Bruce Lathrop.

CHARLOTTE: Oh yes. Bruce and Bob. It all comes back now. Well I'm very sorry. But this is a good ad anyway, I think, so just bring it out to my dirigible, and then come on back in and we'll talk about something else for a while. I know, I mean secretary. Sometimes I think I should get my blood sugar checked.

BRUCE: All right, thank you, Mrs. Wallace.

CHARLOTTE: See you next week.

BRUCE: I thought you wanted me to come right back to finish the session.

CHARLOTTE: Oh yes, see you in a few minutes.
(He *exits*)

CHARLOTTE: (*Into intercom*) Marcia, dear, send in the next porpoise please. Wait, I don't mean porpoise, I mean . . .

pony, pekinese, parka, penis, no not that. I'm sorry, Marcia, I'll buzz back when I think of it.

(Puts her hands over her eyes, moves her lips, trying to remember. Lights dim)

ACT I
Scene 4

A restaurant again. Bruce *waiting, looking at his watch. After a bit enter* Prudence.

PRUDENCE: Oh.

BRUCE: Hello again.

PRUDENCE: Hello.

BRUCE: Odd coincidence.

PRUDENCE: Yes.

BRUCE: Are you meeting someone?

PRUDENCE: Well, yes, I am.

BRUCE: Me too.

PRUDENCE: (*Pause; worried*) Are you meeting someone who answered your ad again?

27

BRUCE: Yes I am.

PRUDENCE: I'm answering an ad again too, I'm embarrassed to say.

BRUCE: Never be embarrassed. We're all human.

PRUDENCE: Yes. Well . . . I think I'll wait over here. Excuse me.
(Prudence *crosses to another table, sits down.*
Bruce *looks at her, a thought dawning. He crosses to her*)

PRUDENCE: Yes?

BRUCE: I'm afraid it's crossed my mind that you answered my ad again.

PRUDENCE: I would not be so stupid as to answer the same ad twice.

BRUCE: I changed my ad.
(She *stares at him*)

BRUCE: I was hoping to get a different sort of person.

PRUDENCE: Are you then the Pulitzer Prize winning author, 6'4", who likes Kierkegaard, Mahler and Joan Didion?

BRUCE: Yes I am. Sorry.

PRUDENCE: I see. Well that was a ludicrous list of people to like anyway. It serves me right.

BRUCE: I'm sorry. It's really just bad luck that it's you again.

PRUDENCE: Thank you very much.

BRUCE: Rather I mean bad luck for you too. That it's me, I mean.

PRUDENCE: I feel so stupid. Do you think we're the only two people who answer these ads?

BRUCE: I doubt it. (*Deciding to try her again*) Maybe we're fated.

PRUDENCE: Jinxed seems more like it.

BRUCE: You think you're unlucky, don't you? In general I mean.
(He *sits down*)

PRUDENCE: You're going to sit down, are you?

BRUCE: Well what else should I do? Go home to Bob?

PRUDENCE: Oh yes. How is Bob?

BRUCE: He's kind of grumpy these days.

PRUDENCE: Perhaps he's having his period.

BRUCE: I don't know much about menstruation. Tell me about it.

PRUDENCE: (*Stares at him*) Yes, I do think I'm unlucky.

BRUCE: What?

PRUDENCE: In answer to your question. I mean, I am attractive, aren't I? I mean, without being conceited, I know I'm fairly attractive. I would think I would have an easy enough time finding someone intelligent and nice, but I only meet creeps.

BRUCE: Thank you very much.

PRUDENCE: Well you're not really a creep, you're more a crackpot.

BRUCE: You're never going to have a successful relationship if you insult people.

PRUDENCE: I'm sorry, I guess I am insulting, but aren't you a crackpot? I mean, from the last time I remember you weep easily, you have some sort of male lover, you want to take terrified children into Plato's Retreat. I mean, don't you think I'm an idiot to stay at this table with you?

BRUCE: I think you're an idiot to be so harsh on people. It must make you very lonely.

PRUDENCE: It does. It makes me very lonely. I mean, do you think it's possible that I am the *only* sane person in the world?

BRUCE: What's so wonderful about being sane? "You must have *madness*," Zorba the Greek says.

PRUDENCE: To whom? Sylvia Plath?

BRUCE: You really don't like me, do you?

PRUDENCE: I don't know you really. (*Pause*) Well, no, I probably don't like you.

BRUCE: (*Getting depressed*) You think I'm not masculine enough probably, don't you?

PRUDENCE: Well I wouldn't say that.

BRUCE: No, I can tell. Women always look at me, and I can hear them disapproving of me because I don't swagger. The stupid John Wayne syndrome.

PRUDENCE: Really it has nothing to do with masculinity. You seem perfectly normal to me. On the surface at least.

BRUCE: Thank you. You have lovely hair.

PRUDENCE: Do I?

BRUCE: You don't know how to accept a compliment.

PRUDENCE: It's just so pretentious to stare soulfully at someone and say you have lovely hair. I mean, do you get results
with men that way?

BRUCE: You're making fun of me.

PRUDENCE: No, I'm not really. I'm just confused. About this
Bob. I mean, if you're living with him, why are you trying
to meet a woman?

BRUCE: I want to be open to all experiences.

PRUDENCE: Well that sounds all very well, but surely you
can't just turn on and off sexual preference.

BRUCE: I don't have to turn it on or off. I prefer both sexes.

PRUDENCE: I don't know, I just find that so difficult to believe.

BRUCE: But why would I be here with you if I weren't interested in you?

PRUDENCE: You might be trying to murder me. Or punish
your mother.

BRUCE: Or I might just be trying to reach out and touch
someone.

PRUDENCE: That's the slogan of Coke or Dr. Pepper, I think.

BRUCE: The telephone company actually. But it's a good slogan. I mean, isn't that what we're all trying to do, reach out to another person? I mean, I put an ad in a newspaper, after all, and you answered it.

PRUDENCE: I know. It's very hard to meet people. I mean I do meet people at the magazine, but they're never right. I met Shaun Cassidy last week. Of course, he's too young for me.

BRUCE: Bob really likes Shaun Cassidy.

PRUDENCE: Oh, I'll have to try to set them up.

BRUCE: How come a pretty girl like you hasn't been married?

PRUDENCE: Oh what a cute question. How come a pretty girl like *you* hasn't been married?

BRUCE: I was married. Right out of high school, I married this girl Sally I knew all through grammar school and everything. We were married for 6 years.

PRUDENCE: Oh. Why did you break up?

BRUCE: I didn't understand about bisexuality then. I thought the fact that I wanted to sleep with the man who came to read the gas meter meant I was queer.

PRUDENCE: I'm never home when they come to read the gas meter.

BRUCE: I blame it on the nuns really. Sisters of Mercy. I mean, they didn't tell us anything about bisexuality.

PRUDENCE: They didn't?

BRUCE: And so then Sally found out I was sleeping with the gas man, and she got real angry. And I didn't know enough then to know that what I felt was perfectly normal; and that really it's very *nice* if I was attracted to both my wife and to the gas man.

PRUDENCE: Mmmm.

BRUCE: So we took me to this very repressive psychiatrist who thought I was *really* sick. And he put me in the hospital and gave me a brain scan. And after that I saw him twice a week to find out what was wrong with me; and every two weeks Sally made me go see this priest who lectured me and read to me from the Book of Leviticus.

PRUDENCE: I don't know the book of Leviticus really.

BRUCE: Oh, it's this really terrific book in the Bible that says that if two men sleep together they should be put to death, and that you shouldn't eat any animals with cloven hoofs or who chew their cud, and then they have this long list of animals; and then all about how women who have their periods are unclean for seven days and if you touch them you have to go wash yourselves, and you can't sit down in a chair they've used or anything. It's a really good book.

PRUDENCE: And what happened to Sally?

BRUCE: Well, she was real mad at me, I guess. So she fell in love with the manager at the A&P, and we got a divorce. So then I came to New York and I got a better therapist who made me see what I felt was perfectly fine. And I've really been much happier. Although Sally still hates me.

PRUDENCE: Hmmmmmmmm.

BRUCE: What about you?

PRUDENCE: What?

BRUCE: What about your life?

33

PRUDENCE: Oh. Well I haven't been married. I could've married this basketball player boyfriend I had in high school. Paul, Paul Rennard. My mother wanted me to marry him. He was very tall. He drank a lot of milk, and wore sweat socks. And then we went to the same college, and we sort of got engaged. No one else had asked me, and my mother thought it was a good idea. But then after being engaged for a year, I realized I really didn't want to marry him. I kept thinking I should break it off but I couldn't.

BRUCE: Why not?

PRUDENCE: Well I didn't want to hurt his feelings. I was afraid he'd realize how *much* I didn't want to marry him.

BRUCE: But you finally told him?

PRUDENCE: Well I realized it was bad to marry someone out of politeness. So after putting it off for months and months, I finally told him. I was very gentle and sweet about it, but when he said I shouldn't make any quick decisions, I sort of lost control and started to shout at him. He was very taken aback. And then offended. He said he was going to join a monastery, which was silly, I don't think they have Unitarian monasteries. But in any case, I wasn't going to have to be Mrs. Paul Rennard, thank goodness.

BRUCE: Have you ever seen a therapist?

PRUDENCE: Yes. I'm seeing one now.

BRUCE: Oh I'm glad. And what happened after college?

PRUDENCE: Well I went to journalism school, and my mother kept calling up saying, why won't you marry Paul? It drove me crazy, but then she finally stopped.

BRUCE: How come?

PRUDENCE: Well he married my younger sister.

BRUCE: How odd.

PRUDENCE: I thought so. I mean no reason he shouldn't. I didn't want to marry him. They have 2.8 children.
(Bruce *looks confused*)

PRUDENCE: She's pregnant.

BRUCE: Oh. Well, who else did you go out with?

PRUDENCE: Well for a while I was afraid if I went out with anyone more than two times, I'd have to marry them, so I never saw anyone for long. But I realized I was getting silly, and that you didn't have to marry anyone unless you *wanted* to. (*Kidding*) Or unless you went out with them *four* times.

BRUCE: Well what else?

PRUDENCE: Then I came to New York, and . . . oh I don't want to go on. I lived happily ever after.

BRUCE: Has there been anyone serious?

PRUDENCE: I have two cats. Serious, let's see. Well my boss at *Newsweek*, that was serious. He was married, but he said he couldn't get a divorce because his wife was hopelessly insane like in *Jane Eyre*. I should've known better. She wasn't insane, she was in the Bahamas. It took me several months to break that off, I was afraid he'd fire me. So finally I just quit, and I went to work for *Time*. And then at *Time* I met Howard, who seemed sweet but turned out to be a lunatic.

BRUCE: How, a lunatic?

PRUDENCE: Well, he was a twin and started to think he was his brother. And when his brother came to visit, then he didn't know who he was. So after that I kind of gave up trying to have relationships for a while, and I went to work for *People*.

BRUCE: You shouldn't be so afraid of trying.

PRUDENCE: Well you never met Howard. I did have one pretty good relationship.

BRUCE: (*Warmly*) I'm glad.

PRUDENCE: (*A touch satirically*) Thank you. About a year and a half ago I lived for six months with this aging preppie named Michael.

BRUCE: I'm an aging preppie.

PRUDENCE: (*Smiles*) Yes I know. Michael was a lawyer, and he was very smart, and very nice; and I should've been happy with him, and I don't know why I wasn't. And he was slightly allergic to my cats, and so I took that to be an omen of some sort, so I broke it off.

BRUCE: And you haven't gone out with anyone since?

PRUDENCE: Well I do go out with people, but it never seems to work out.

BRUCE: I bet you're too hard on them. I bet the second night you decide they're dull or a lunatic, and then you just give up on them.

PRUDENCE: Well I guess I do sound judgmental, but why shouldn't I be? I mean, should I pretend someone is wonderful if I think they're stupid or crazy?

BRUCE: Well no, but it sounds like you judge everybody too quickly.

PRUDENCE: Well perhaps. But how many nights would you give David Berkowitz?

BRUCE: You went out with David Berkowitz?

PRUDENCE: No. It was a rhetorical question.

BRUCE: But don't you want to get married?

PRUDENCE: I have no idea. It's so confusing. I know when I was a little girl, Million Dollar Movie showed this film called *Every Girl Should Be Married* every night for seven days. It was this dumb comedy about this girl played by Betsy Drake who wants to be married to this man played by Cary Grant who she sees in a drug store. She sees him for two minutes and she wants to have babies and move in with him. But he finds her obnoxious and he tells her so, but then for the whole rest of the movie she chases and chases after him, and then at the end he says, "Ok, I give in, you're adorable." And then they get married. (*Looks baffled by the stupidity of it all*)

BRUCE: Well it was a comedy.

PRUDENCE: And what confused me further was that the actress, Betsy Drake, did in fact marry Cary Grant in real life. Of course it didn't last, and he married several other people, and then later Dyan Cannon said he was insane and took LSD, and so maybe one wouldn't want to be married to him at all. But if it's no good being married to Cary Grant, who is it good being married to?

BRUCE: I don't know.

PRUDENCE: Neither do I.
(*Pause*)

BRUCE: Well, you should give things time. First impressions can be wrong. And maybe Dyan Cannon was the problem. Maybe anyone married to her would take LSD. Maybe Cary Grant is still terrific.

PRUDENCE: Well I don't want to talk about movie stars anymore.

BRUCE: No, you're right.

PRUDENCE: What do you do for a living? I never asked you.

BRUCE: I sell mutual bonds. Would you like to buy some?

PRUDENCE: No. I don't really understand about mutual bonds. But please don't explain them to me now. I don't want to know.

BRUCE: You're so afraid of things. I feel this overwhelming urge to help you. We can look into the abyss together.

PRUDENCE: Oh please don't keep saying pretentious things. I'll get a rash.

BRUCE: You're right. I guess I am pretentious. (*Depressed*)

PRUDENCE: Well I really am too hard on people.

BRUCE: No you're probably right to dislike me. Sally hates me. I mean, sometimes I hear myself and I understand why no one likes me.

PRUDENCE: Please don't be so hard on yourself on my account. Everyone's stupid, so you're just like everyone else.
(He *stares at her*)

PRUDENCE: I'm sorry, that sounded terrible, I'm stupid too. We're all stupid.

BRUCE: It's human to be stupid. (*Sings romantically*)
There's a somebody I'm longing duh duh
Duh duh duh duh, duh duh duh dum . . .

PRUDENCE: (*Sings*) Someone to watch . . . (*Realizes* she's *singing alone*) Oh I didn't realize you were stopping.

BRUCE: Sorry. I didn't realize you were . . . starting.

PRUDENCE: Yes. Stupid of me to like that song.

BRUCE: It's a pretty song.

PRUDENCE: Well I guess it is.

BRUCE: I like you.

PRUDENCE: Do you?

BRUCE: You still don't know how to accept a compliment.

PRUDENCE: Well . . .

BRUCE: Just say thank you.
(She *looks embarrassed*)

BRUCE: Really, just say thank you.

PRUDENCE: Very well. Thank you.

BRUCE: I do like you. I like women who are independent-minded, who don't look to a man to do all their thinking for them. I like women who are persons.

PRUDENCE: Well you sound like you were coached by Betty Friedan, but otherwise that's a nice sentiment. Of course, a woman who was independent-minded wouldn't like the song "Someone to Watch Over Me."

BRUCE: We have to allow for contradictions in ourselves. Nobody is just one thing.

PRUDENCE: (*Serious*) That's very true. That wasn't a crackpot comment at all.

BRUCE: I know it wasn't. And just because I'm a crackpot on some things doesn't mean I'm a total crackpot. In many regards I may be a fine and sensitive person, but you'll never find out if you close yourself off before you get to know me on the basis of a few crackpot comments.

PRUDENCE: Well that's true too. Not as true as what you said before, but true too.

BRUCE: I do like you. Do you like me?

PRUDENCE: Well I don't know. I don't really know you yet.

BRUCE: Do you want to get to know me?

PRUDENCE: I don't know. Maybe I shouldn't. I mean, we did meet through a personal ad, you don't have a Pulitzer Prize . . .

BRUCE: I have a membership in the New York Health and Racquet Club.

PRUDENCE: Well similar, but not the same thing.

BRUCE: As a member I can get you a discount.

PRUDENCE: I don't know if I'm ready to exercise yet. I'm thinking about it, but I'm cautious still.

BRUCE: We're getting on, aren't we?

PRUDENCE: Well yes, in a way. (*Looks around*) Do you think maybe they don't have waiters in this restaurant?

BRUCE: Maybe they're on strike. Why don't we go to another restaurant? I know a good Mexican one.

PRUDENCE: I don't like Mexican food, I'm afraid.

BRUCE: Japanese?

PRUDENCE: Well no.

BRUCE: Chinese?

PRUDENCE: Well more than Japanese, but not really.

BRUCE: Where do you want to go?

PRUDENCE: Well could we go to an American restaurant? I know I'm very dull, but I didn't even like vanilla ice cream when I was a child. I was afraid of it.

BRUCE: That's a significant statement you've just made.

PRUDENCE: It does sound pathological, doesn't it?

BRUCE: Don't be afraid to sound pathological. That's what I've learned from my therapy so far.

PRUDENCE: (*Curious*) What kind of therapy are you in? One of the crackpot specialties? Oh I'm sorry, I'm being judgmental again. I just thought you probably wouldn't be in "regular" therapy, but one of those nut specialties. I'm sorry, I'm *trying* not to be judgmental. Let me try again. Are you in a "unique" form of therapy?

BRUCE: Unique is a good word. (*As they walk out*) We're all unique, Prudence.
(They *exit*)

ACT I
Scene 5

Dr. Stuart Framingham's *office again.*

STUART: (*On phone*) Hiya, babe, it's me. Whatcha doin'? Oh, I'm just waiting for my next patient. Last night was great, wasn't it? It was great. What? So quickly. What is it with you women? You read some goddamned sex manual and then you think sex is supposed to go on for hours or something? I mean, if you're so frigid you can't get excited in a couple of minutes, that's not my problem. No it isn't. Well, fuck you too. (*Hangs up*) Jesus God. (*Into intercom*) Betty, you can send in the next patient.
(*Enter* Prudence. She *sits*)

STUART: Hello.

PRUDENCE: Hello.

STUART: What's on your mind this week?

PRUDENCE: Nothing.

43

STUART: Goddamn it. I don't feel like dragging the words out of you this week. Talk, damn it. (She *stares at him*)

PRUDENCE: What?

STUART: You pay me to listen, so TALK! I'm sorry, I'm on edge today. And all my patients are this way. None of them talk. Well this one guy talks, but he talks in Yiddish a lot, and I don't know what the fuck he's saying.

PRUDENCE: Well you should tell him that you don't understand.

STUART: Don't tell me how to run my business! Besides, we're here to talk about you. How was your week? Another series of lonely, loveless evenings? I'm still here, babe.

PRUDENCE: Don't call me babe. No, I've had some pleasant evenings actually.

STUART: You have?

PRUDENCE: Yes I have.

STUART: You been answering ads in the paper again?

PRUDENCE: Well, yes actually.

STUART: That's a slutty thing to do.

PRUDENCE: As a therapist you are utterly ridiculous.

STUART: I'm just kidding you. You shouldn't lose your sense of humor, babe, especially when you're in a promiscuous stage.

PRUDENCE: I am not promiscuous.

STUART: There's nothing wrong with being promiscuous. We're all human.

PRUDENCE: Yes, we are all human.

STUART: So who is this guy? Have you slept with him?

PRUDENCE: Dr. Framingham . . .

STUART: Really, I gotta know for therapy.

PRUDENCE: Yes, we have slept together. Once. I wasn't really planning to, but . . .

STUART: Is he better than me?

PRUDENCE: Stuart . . .

STUART: No really. You liked him better? Tell me.

PRUDENCE: Yes I did. Much better.

STUART: I suppose he took his time. I suppose it lasted just hours. That's sick! Wanting sex to take a long time is sick!

PRUDENCE: Well he was attentive to how I felt, if that's what you mean.

STUART: So this fellow was a real success, huh?

PRUDENCE: Success and failure are not particularly likable terms to describe sexual outings, but if you must, yes, it was successful. Probably his experiences with men have made him all that better as a lover.

STUART: What?

PRUDENCE: He's bisexual.

STUART: (*Starting to feel on the winning team again*) Oh yeah?

PRUDENCE: So he tells me. Masters and Johnson say that homosexuals make much more responsive sex partners anyway.

STUART: BULLSHIT! You are talking such bullshit! I understand you now. You're obviously afraid of a real man, and so you want to cuddle with some eunuch who isn't a threat to you. I understand all this now!

PRUDENCE: There's no need to call him a eunuch. A eunuch has no testicles.

STUART: I GOT BALLS, BABY!

PRUDENCE: I am so pleased for you. Have you written into the *Guinness Book of Records* yet?

STUART: You're afraid of men!

PRUDENCE: I am not afraid of men. Rather I don't like men when they are idiotic and boorish, which is what you are.

STUART: You're a fag hag. (*Writes that down, makes further notes*)

PRUDENCE: Look, I admit I find this man's supposed bisexuality confusing and I don't quite believe it; and I also think he's probably an emotional and intellectual nut, but so far his competition for my interest is almost nonexistent. What are my options? A two-minute roll in the hay with you, where you make no distinction between sexual intercourse and push-ups; and then a happy evening of admiring your underarm hair and your belt buckles? (*Irritated*) What are you writing?

STUART: (*Reading from his pad*) I'd like to give this patient electro-shock therapy. I'd like to put this patient in a clothes dryer until her hair falls out. I'd like to tie her to the radiator and . . . (*Stops, hears himself, looks stricken*)

PRUDENCE: I think this is obviously my last session.

STUART: No, no, no. You're taking me seriously. I'm testing you. It was a test. I was just putting you on.

PRUDENCE: For what purpose?

STUART: I can't tell you. It would interfere with your therapy.

PRUDENCE: You call this therapy?

STUART: We're reaching the richest part of our therapy. And already I see results. You never used to be able to express your anger so openly.

PRUDENCE: Well anyone can be goaded into anger, that's not a change.

STUART: It *is* a change. I've helped you. But I think you're entering a very unchartered part of your life just now, and so you must stay with your therapy. You're going out with homosexuals. God knows what you're going to do next. Now I'm very serious. I'm holding out the lifeline. Don't turn away.

PRUDENCE: Well I'll think about it, but I don't know.

STUART: You're a very sick woman, and you mustn't be without a therapist even for a day.

PRUDENCE: (*Not taken in by this; wanting to leave without a scene*) Is the session over yet?

STUART: We have thirty more minutes.

PRUDENCE: Could I go early?

STUART: I think it's important that we finish out the session.

PRUDENCE: I'd like to go.

STUART: Please, please, please, please . . .

PRUDENCE: All right, all right. For God's sake.
(They *settle down, back in their chairs*)

STUART: When are you seeing this person again? I'm asking as your therapist.

PRUDENCE: Tonight. He's making dinner for us.

STUART: *He*'s making dinner?

PRUDENCE: He says he likes to cook.

STUART: I don't think I need say anything more.

PRUDENCE: I don't think you do either.
(They *stare at one another; lights dim*)

ACT I

Scene 6

Bruce's *apartment*. Bruce *fiddling with pillows, on couch, looking at watch, etc. Doorbell.*

BRUCE:
(*Letting in* Prudence)
Hi. Come on in.

PRUDENCE: Hello. I brought some wine.

BRUCE: Oh thanks.

PRUDENCE: You have a nice apartment.

BRUCE: Thanks.

PRUDENCE: It looks just like my apartment.

BRUCE: Yeah I guess it does.

PRUDENCE: And like my therapist's office. And like my office at the magazine. Everything looks alike.

49

BRUCE: I guess everyone has the same taste in furniture.

PRUDENCE: I don't think I know anyone who has an oriental rug.

BRUCE: They are expensive.

PRUDENCE: My mother's house has an oriental rug. Her furnishings don't look anything like this.

BRUCE: No?

PRUDENCE: I'm sorry, I'm just rattling on.

BRUCE: That's all right. Sit down.
(They *sit*)

PRUDENCE: It's really very nice of you to cook.

BRUCE: Well I thought it would be a good way of making sure that we didn't start by acting out any sexual stereotyping. No woman-does-the-cooking, man-carves-the-roast-beef sort of thing.

PRUDENCE: Oh, are we having roast beef?

BRUCE: Well, no actually. Lamb chops.

PRUDENCE: Well no carving there.

BRUCE: Right. Can I get you a drink?

PRUDENCE: Ummm, I don't know.

BRUCE: Do you want one?

PRUDENCE: I don't know. Do you want one?

BRUCE: Well I thought I might have some Perrier.

PRUDENCE: Oh that sounds good.

BRUCE: Two Perriers?

PRUDENCE: Well, do you have Poland water?

BRUCE: I think I do. Wait here. I'll be right back.
(Bruce *exits. After a moment* Bob *enters.* Bob *sees* Prudence, *is rattled, ill at ease*)

BOB: Oh. You're here already. I . . . didn't hear the bell ring.

PRUDENCE: Oh. Hello. Are you Bob?

BOB: Yes. (*At a loss*) And you must be Marie of Roumania.

PRUDENCE: I'm Prudence.

BOB: Yes, I know. (*At a loss how to get out of room*) Is Bruce in the kitchen?

PRUDENCE: Yes.

BOB: Oh. (*Starts to go there*) Oh, well, never mind. When he comes out would you tell him I want to see him in the other room?

PRUDENCE: All right.

BOB: Excuse me.
(*Exits back to bedroom presumably.*
Enter Bruce *with two glasses of water*)

BRUCE: Well here we are. One Perrier, and one Poland water.

PRUDENCE: I thought you said Bob was away.

BRUCE: Oh, you met Bob already? Yes, he *was* going away, but then he changed his mind, and I'd already bought the lamb chops.

PRUDENCE: You mean he's going to be here all through dinner?

BRUCE: Oh I don't think so. He said he was going to his mother's for dinner. He has a very funny mother. She's sort of like Auntie Mame.

PRUDENCE: Oh, yes?

BRUCE: Now don't let Bob upset you.

PRUDENCE: Well he seemed very uncomfortable. He asked me if I was Marie of Roumania.

BRUCE: Oh he always says that. Don't take it personally. (*Raising drink*) Well, cheers.

PRUDENCE: (*Remembering*) Oh. He said he wanted to see you in the other room.

BRUCE: Oh. Well, all right. I'll just be a minute. Here, why don't you read a magazine?

PRUDENCE: *People*, how nice.

BRUCE: Be right back.
(*Exits. Prudence reads magazine uncomfortably, and/or also might taste his Perrier water to compare it with her Poland water. We and she start to hear the following Offstage argument; initially it's just a buzz of voices, but it grows into anger and shouting. Prudence looks very uncomfortable*)

BRUCE: (*Offstage*) This isn't the time to talk about this, Bob.

BOB: (*Offstage*) Well, when is the time?

BRUCE: (*Offstage*) We can talk about this later.

BOB: (*Offstage*) That's obviously very convenient for you.

BRUCE: (*Offstage*) Bob, this isn't the time to talk about this.

BOB: (*Offstage*) Well when *is* the time?

BRUCE: (*Offstage*) Come on, Bob, calm down. (*Softer*) Now I told you this doesn't have anything to do with us.

BOB: (*Offstage. Very angry*) Oh God!

BRUCE: (*Offstage*) I'm sick of this behavior, Bob!

BOB: (*Offstage*) Well I'm sick of it too!
(*There is a crash of something breaking. Pause. Then re-enter* Bruce)

BRUCE: Everything's fine now. (*Pause*) We broke a vase. Well Bob broke it.

PRUDENCE: Maybe I should go.

BRUCE: No, everything's fine now. Once Bob vents his anger then everything's fine again.

PRUDENCE: Oh well, that's good.

BRUCE: This is difficult for Bob, but he said he was going to be civilized about it.

PRUDENCE: I thought you told me that Bob didn't mind about your seeing me. And that the two of you had broken up anyway.

BRUCE: Well, I lied. Sorry. Some members of Bob's group therapy wrote me a note saying they thought if I wanted to see women, I should just go on and see women, and so I just sort of presumed they'd convince Bob eventually. But I guess they haven't yet.

PRUDENCE: They wrote you a letter?

BRUCE: It's a very intense group Bob is in. They're always visiting each other in the hospital and things.

PRUDENCE: But what shall we do about this evening?

BRUCE: Well really, I think you and Bob will really like one another once you get past this initial discomfort. And he is going to his mother's.

PRUDENCE: Maybe we should go to a restaurant.

BRUCE: No really, I bought the lamb chops. It'll be fine. Oh my God, the rice. I have to go see about the rice. It's wild rice; well, Rice-A-Roni. I have to go see about browning it. I won't be a minute.

PRUDENCE: No, no, don't leave . . .

BRUCE: It's all right. (*As* he *leaves*) Bob will come talk to you . . .
(*Exits*)

PRUDENCE: (*As* she *sees* he's *gone*) I know . . . Oh dear.
(*Enter* Bob)

BOB: Hello again.

PRUDENCE: Oh hi.

54

BOB: I didn't mean to make you uncomfortable about Marie of Roumania. It's just something I say.

PRUDENCE: Oh that's all right.

BOB: (*Offering it as information*) I just broke a vase.

PRUDENCE: (*Being pleasant*) Oh yes, I thought I heard something.

BOB: Bruce says that I will like you if I can just get past my initial hostility.

PRUDENCE: Oh. Well I hope so.

BOB: Bruce is really a very conflicted person. I really suffer a lot dealing with him.

PRUDENCE: Oh I'm sorry.

BOB: And now this latest thing of having women traipse through here at all hours.

PRUDENCE: Ah.

BOB: Did you ever see the movie *Sunday Bloody Sunday?*

PRUDENCE: No I didn't. I meant to.

BOB: Well I sure wish Bruce had never seen it. It had a big effect on him. It's all about this guy played by Murray Head who's having an affair with Peter Finch *and* with Glenda Jackson.

PRUDENCE: Oh. Good actors.

BOB: That's not really the point. The point is that it's a very silly movie because I don't think bisexuality exists, do you?

PRUDENCE: Well it's hard to know really.

BOB: I mean, I think that Bruce is just trying to prove something with all these ads in the paper for women. That's what my mother says about Bruce. She tells me I should just be patient and understanding and that it's just a phase Bruce is going through. I've put a lot of work into this relationship. And it's so difficult meeting new people, it's just thoroughly intimidating.

PRUDENCE: It is hard to meet people.

BOB: I think everyone is basically gay, don't you?

PRUDENCE: Well, no, not really.

BOB: You just say that because you haven't come out yet. I know lots of lesbians who'd like you a lot. I'd be happy to give them your number.

PRUDENCE: Thank you, but no.
(*Enter* Bruce)

BRUCE: Well I burned the rice. Sorry. We'll just have more salad.

PRUDENCE: Oh that's all right.

BRUCE: So have you two been getting to know one another?

PRUDENCE: Yes.

BOB: (*Truly being conversational, not trying to be rude. To* Bruce) Don't you think Prudence would be a big hit in a lesbian bar?

BRUCE: Yes, I guess she would.

BOB: I know Liz Skinner would certainly like her.

BRUCE: Yes, she is Liz's type.

PRUDENCE: Bruce, could I speak to you for a moment please? (*To* Bob) I'm sorry, excuse me.
(Bruce *and* Prudence *cross to side of room*)

PRUDENCE: Bruce, I'm getting very uncomfortable. Now you told me that Bob wasn't going to be here and that he wasn't jealous about your seeing women, and I don't want to be told which lesbians would like me, and furthermore I'm not interested in acting out scenes from . . . (*To* Bob) What's the name of that movie you mentioned again?

BOB: *Sunday Bloody Sunday.*

PRUDENCE: (*To* Bruce) And I'm not interested in acting out scenes from *Sunday Bloody Sunday.* (*To* Bob) Thank you. (*Back to* Bruce) So I think maybe I should forget the whole thing and go home.

BRUCE: No please, don't go. Bob needs help to get over his feelings about this, and he is trying to be pleasant. And he has a real problem with women anyway, so you can be enormously helpful to him if you make him think you like him. And besides, I'm sure he'll go to his mother's in a little while. So please just be nice to him for a little longer. For our sake.

PRUDENCE: I don't know.

BRUCE: Really, it'll be fine.
(They *return to* Bob)

PRUDENCE: (*On returning, to* Bob) Sorry.

BOB: Don't be sorry. I realize I make you uncomfortable.

PRUDENCE: No, no, really it's not that.

57

BRUCE: Prudence likes you, Bob. She isn't like the other women you know.

PRUDENCE: Yes, I do . . . I like lots of men. (*Laughs nervously*)

BOB: We have that in common.

PRUDENCE: Yes . . . (*Laughs, very uncomfortable*)

BRUCE: (*Making big transition into "conversation"*) So, Prudence, did you finish writing your interview with Joyce De Witt?

BOB: Who's Joyce De Witt?

PRUDENCE: (*Trying to be very friendly*) Oh, she's the brunette actress on the TV show "Three's a Crowd." (*Pause; looks mortified*) I mean, "Three's Company."
(*Long pause. They all feel awful*)

BRUCE: So, did you finish the article?

PRUDENCE: Yes. I did. Right on time. (*Pause; to* Bob) Bruce tells me your mother is like Auntie Mame.
(Bob *glares at* Bruce)

PRUDENCE: Oh, I'm sorry. Was that a bad thing to say?

BOB: It depends on what you mean by Auntie Mame.

PRUDENCE: I don't know. Bruce said it.

BOB: My mother has a certain flair, if that's what he means.

BRUCE: Your mother acts like a transvestite. I'm sorry, she does.

58

BOB: Just because my mother has a sense of humor is no reason to accuse her of not being feminine. (*To Prudence*) Don't you agree that women *theoretically* can have senses of humor?

PRUDENCE: Yes indeed.

BRUCE: Sense of humor isn't the issue.
(*Pause*)

PRUDENCE: (*Trying to help conversation*) I've always hated transvestites. It's such a repugnant image of women.
(Bob *looks disapproving*)

PRUDENCE: I'm sorry, I don't mean to imply anything about your mother. I . . . I liked Jack Lemmon as a woman in *Some Like It Hot*.

BOB: My mother does not resemble Jack Lemmon in *Some Like It Hot*.

PRUDENCE: I'm sure she doesn't. I didn't mean to imply . . . I don't know what I meant to imply . . .

BRUCE: Change the subject, Prudence. This is getting us nowhere.

PRUDENCE: Oh, all right. (*Thinks*) What does Bob do for a living?

BOB: I'm still in the room.

PRUDENCE: Oh I'm sorry, I know you are. I didn't mean to put the question in the third person. I was just thinking of it as a topic rather than a question. (*Pause*) And so I ended up putting it in the third person. (*Pause*) What do you do for a living, Bob?

BOB: I'm a pharmacist.

PRUDENCE: Oh really?

BOB: Do you need any pills?

PRUDENCE: No thank you. (*Pause*) Maybe later.

BRUCE: (*To* Prudence) Can I freshen your Poland water?

PRUDENCE: No thank you. I'm fine. (*Pause*) The Pope is Polish now.

BOB: Now? You mean he wasn't before?

PRUDENCE: No. I just mean the previous one wasn't.

BRUCE: I was brought up by nuns. They really wrecked me.

BOB: They certainly did.
(*Pause*)

PRUDENCE: So you're a pharmacist.

BOB: Yes.

BRUCE: I wish I hadn't burned the rice. (*Whispers to* Prudence) Say something to him, he's starting to sulk.

PRUDENCE: Ummmm . . . What exactly is in Tylenol, I wonder.

BOB: That's all right. I realize I'm making everyone uncomfortable. Excuse me. (*Exits*)

PRUDENCE: Really, Bruce, this isn't very fair to me. This is a problem the two of you should work out together.

BRUCE: Well you're right actually. You're always right. That's why I like you so much. (*Moves closer, puts arm around her*)

PRUDENCE: Maybe I should go.

BRUCE: Oh you're too sensitive. Besides, he'll be leaving soon. (Bob *re-enters*)

BOB: My mother's on the phone.

BRUCE: I didn't hear it ring.

BOB: I called her. (*To* Prudence) She wants to speak to you.

PRUDENCE: I don't understand. I . . .

BOB: (*Hands her the phone*) Here.

PRUDENCE: (*It's happening too fast to stop*) Hello. Who is this? Oh, hello. Yes. (*Laughs uncomfortably*) Yes, thank you. What? No, I don't want to ruin your son's life. What? No, really, I'm not trying to . . .

BRUCE: (*Takes phone away from* Prudence; *talks into it*) Now, look, Sadie. I've told you not to meddle in my life. It doesn't do anybody any good when you do, including Bob. Don't sing when I'm talking to you, that's not communication to sing when someone is talking to you. Sadie . . . Sadie! (*Hands phone to* Bob) She's singing "Rose's Turn" from *Gypsy*, it's utterly terrifying.

BOB: Hello, Mother.

BRUCE: (*To* Prudence) She's an insane woman.

BOB: Mother, it's me, you can stop singing now. Okay, well, just finish the phrase. (*Listens*)

PRUDENCE: Where's Bob's father?

BRUCE: She killed him.

BOB: That's not funny, Bruce. Okay, Mother, wrap the song up now. Yes, I'm all right. Yes, I'll tell them. (*To the* two of them) My mother thinks you're both very immature, (*Back to phone*) Yes, I think she's a lesbian too. But Bruce is just afraid of closeness, just like everybody said in group last week. (*To* Prudence) Nobody in group likes Bruce at all.

BRUCE: I don't think group therapy is helping Bob. It's too unstructured.

BOB: (*To phone*) I don't know if I feel ready to leave Bruce yet, Mother.

PRUDENCE: I'm going to go home now.

BRUCE: No, no, I'll fix this. (*Takes phone away from* BOB) Finish this conversation in the other room, Bob. Then please get out of here, as we agreed you would do earlier, so Prudence and I can have our dinner. I mean, we agreed upon this, Bob.

BOB: You mean you agreed upon it.

BRUCE: I've finished with this conversation, Bob. Go in the other room and talk to your mother. (*Listens to phone*) What's she singing now, I don't recognize it?

BOB: That's "Welcome to Kanagawa" from *Pacific Overtures*.

BRUCE: Keep singing, Sadie. Bob is changing phones. It was good hearing from you.

Bruce (Stephen Collins), having known Prudence (Sigourney Weaver) for all of ten minutes, is already imagining himself in love with her.

"In some ways you're like a little girl. And in some ways you're like a woman," he tells her.

"How am I like a woman?" she asks.

Searchingly, romantically, he answers, "You...dress like a woman. You wear eye shadow like a woman."

She, returning in kind, thinks he's "like a man. You're tall, you have to shave...."

Bruce sees his off-the-wall shrink, Charlotte Wallace (left in photo; played by Kate McGregor-Stewart), who hugs her stuffed dog and asks probing analytical questions.

"I threw a glass of water at someone in a restaurant," Bruce admits during one of their sessions.

"Did they get all wet?" Charlotte queries.

BRUCE: I'm deeply emotional. I like to cry.
PRUDENCE: Oh I wouldn't like that.
BRUCE: But I *like* to cry.
PRUDENCE: I don't think men should cry unless something falls on them.

BRUCE: We have to talk this through.
PRUDENCE: Bruce.
BOB: I don't want to talk it through.
(Sings) Frères Jacques, Frères Jacques, dormez-vous?
dormez-vous? (Etc., continues on)
PRUDENCE: Bruce.
BRUCE: Don't sing when I'm talking to you.

photographs by Martha Swope

BOB: I just don't understand your behavior. I just don't. (*Exits*)

PRUDENCE: I can't tell you how uncomfortable I am. Really I must go home, and then the two of you should go to a marriage counselor or something.

BRUCE: I am sorry. I should have protected you from this. (*Listens to phone, hangs it up*) I mean you must think I'm ridiculous. And really Bob is very nice, we're just going through a difficult period and it makes him act crazy.

PRUDENCE: I mean we're only seeing one another casually, and you and Bob have lived together, and his mother calls up and she sings . . .

BRUCE: I'm not feeling all that casual anymore. Are you?

PRUDENCE: Well I don't know. I mean, probably yes, it's still casual.

BRUCE: It needn't be.

PRUDENCE: Bruce, I just don't think your life is in order.

BRUCE: Of course it's not. How can life be in order? Life by its very nature is disordered, terrifying. That's why people come together, to face the terrors hand in hand.

PRUDENCE: You're giving me my rash again.

BRUCE: You're so afraid of feeling.

PRUDENCE: Maybe you should put the lamb chops on.

BRUCE: I feel very close to you.
(*Enter Bob with suitcase. Phone rings*)

BOB: Don't answer it. It's just my mother again. I told her I was checking into a hotel and then jumping out the window. There's just no point in continuing. (*To Prudence, sincerely*) I hope you're both very happy. Really.

PRUDENCE: (*Startled, confused*) Thank you.

BRUCE: Bob, come back here. (*Answers phone*) Sadie, we'll call you back. (*Hangs up*) Bob.

BOB: No, go back to your evening. I don't want to stand in your way.

BRUCE: You're just trying to get attention.

BOB: There's just no point in continuing.
(*Phone rings; Bruce answers it*)

BRUCE: It's all right, Sadie. I'll handle this (*Hangs up*) Bob, people who announce their suicide are just asking for help, isn't that so, Prudence?

PRUDENCE: I really don't know. I think I should leave.

BOB: No, please, I don't want to spoil your dinner.

BRUCE: You're just asking for help. (*Phone rings*) Let's let it ring. Bob, look at me. I want you to get help. Can you hear me? I want you to see my therapist.

BOB: I have my own group therapy.

BRUCE: You need better help than that. Doesn't he, Prudence? (*Answers phone*) It's all right, Sadie, I'm going to call up my therapist right away. (*Hangs up*) Now you just sit down here, Bob, and we're going to call Mrs. Wallace right up. (*To* Prudence) Unless you think your therapist is better.

PRUDENCE: No! Yours would have to be better.

BOB: I don't know what you have against my group therapy. It's been very helpful to me.

BRUCE: Bob, you're trying to kill yourself. That proves to me that group therapy is a failure. (*Phone rings; answers*) Sadie, we need to keep this line free. Now stop calling for a while. (*Hangs up*)

BOB: It proves no such thing. Suicide is an innate human right. Didn't you see that overweight woman in the *Times* who turned her suicide into a work of art?

BRUCE: She was terminally ill.

BOB: I'm emotionally terminally ill. So I'm making a free choice.
(*Phone rings*)

BRUCE: (*To* Prudence; *hands her phone*) Will you tell her to stop calling?

PRUDENCE: Hello?

BRUCE: You're not acting logically.

PRUDENCE: No, I don't want to see him dead.

BOB: I simply think I should end my life now. That's logical.

PRUDENCE: Please don't shout at me, Mrs. Lansky.

BRUCE: We have to talk this through.

PRUDENCE: Bruce.

BOB: I don't want to talk it through. (*Sings*) Frère Jacques, frère Jacques, dormez-vous? dormez-vous? (*Etc., continues on*)

PRUDENCE: Bruce.

BRUCE: Don't sing when I'm talking to you.

PRUDENCE: Bruce.

BRUCE: What is it, Prudence?

PRUDENCE: Please, Mrs. Lansky is yelling at me.

BRUCE: Well she can't hurt you. Yell back.

BOB: (*Takes phone*) Mother, it's all right. I want to die. (*Hands phone back to* Prudence, *goes back to song*) Ding dong ding ding dong ding. Frère Jacques . . . (*Continues*)

BRUCE: Bob, you're acting like a baby.

PRUDENCE: No, he's still alive, Mrs. Lansky.

BRUCE: (*Irritated, starts to sing at* Bob) Seventy-six trombones led the big parade, with a hundred and ten cornets close behind . . . (*Continues*)

PRUDENCE: Mrs. Lansky, I'm going to hang up now. Goodbye. Stop yelling. (*Hangs up*)

BOB: (*Stops singing*) Did you hang up on my mother? (Bruce *stops too*)

PRUDENCE: Oh why don't you just go kill yourself?
(BOB *sits down, stunned. Phone rings*)

PRUDENCE: (*Answers it*) Oh shut up. (*Hangs up*) I am very uninterested in being involved in this nonsense. You're both just making a big overdramatic mess out of everything, and I don't want to watch it anymore.

BRUCE: You're right. Bob, she's right.

BOB: (*Looks up*) She is?

BRUCE: Yes, she is. We're really acting stupid.
(*Phone rings. Bruce picks it up, and hangs up immediately. Then he dials*)

BRUCE: I'm calling Mrs. Wallace now. I think we really need help.

PRUDENCE: You have her home number?

BRUCE: Yes. She's a really wonderful woman. She gave me her home number after our second session.

PRUDENCE: I slept with my therapist after our second session.

BRUCE: Hello? Uh, is Mrs. Wallace there? Thank you. (*To them*) I think that was her husband.

BOB: (*Not defiantly; just for something to do, sings softly*) Frère Jacques, frère Jacques, dormez-vous . . . (*Etc.*)

BRUCE: (*Suddenly hearing it*) What do you mean you slept with your therapist?

PRUDENCE: I don't know, I . . .

BRUCE: (*To Bob, suddenly*) Sssssh. (*Into phone*) Hello. Mrs. Wallace? Mrs. Wallace, this is Bruce, we have a bit of an emergency, I wonder if you can help . . . we're in desperate need of some therapy here . . .

END ACT I

ACT TWO

ACT II

Scene 1

(Mrs. Wallace's *office, twenty minutes after the end of Act I.* Mrs. Wallace *present, enter* Bruce *and* Bob)

BRUCE: Hi, it's us.

CHARLOTTE: Hello.

BRUCE: Really, it's so nice of you to see us right away.

CHARLOTTE: That's all right.

BRUCE: Mrs. Wallace, this is Bob Lansky.

CHARLOTTE: Hello.

BOB: Hello.

BRUCE: Well I'm going to leave you two and go have dinner with Prudence.

BOB: You're not going to stay?

BRUCE: Bob, you're the one who's not handling this situation well. Now I haven't eaten all day, and this hasn't been fair to Prudence. (*To Mrs. Wallace*) Now if he gets totally out of control, we're going to be at the Squire Restaurant. I mean I could be paged. Otherwise, I'll just see you back at the apartment.

BOB: I thought you wanted her to talk to us together.

BRUCE: Not for the first session. Now you listen to what Mrs. Wallace has to say, and I'll see you later tonight.
(*Gives* Bob *an affectionate hug, then exits.* Bob *and* Mrs. Wallace *stare at one another for a while*)

BOB: Should I sit down?

CHARLOTTE: Would you like to sit down?
(*He sits. She sits, holds her Snoopy doll*)

BOB: Why are you holding that doll?

CHARLOTTE: Does it bother you that I hold the doll?

BOB: I don't know.

CHARLOTTE: Were you allowed to have dolls as a child?

BOB: Yes I was. It was trucks I wasn't allowed to have.

CHARLOTTE: Great big trucks?

BOB: Toy trucks.
(*Silence*)

CHARLOTTE: Now, what seems to be the matter?

BOB: Bruce seems to be trying to end our relationship.

CHARLOTTE: What do you mean?

BOB: He's been putting these ads in the paper for women. And now he seems a little serious about this new one.

CHARLOTTE: Women?

BOB: Women.

CHARLOTTE: And why does this bother you?

BOB: Well, Bruce and I have been living together for a year. A little more.

CHARLOTTE: Living together?

BOB: Yes.

CHARLOTTE: As roommates?

BOB: Well, if that's the euphemism you prefer.

CHARLOTTE: I prefer nothing. I'm here to help you.

BOB: But you can see the problem.

CHARLOTTE: Well, if Bruce should move out, surely you can find another roommate. They advertise in the paper. As a matter of fact, my son is looking for a roommate. He doesn't get on with the present Mr. Wallace. Maybe you could room with him.

BOB: I don't think you've understood. Bruce and I aren't just roommates, you know. I mean, doesn't he talk to you about me in his own therapy?

CHARLOTTE: Let me get his file. (*Looks through her drawers*) No, it's not here. Maybe my dirigible knows where it is.

73

(*Pushes button*) Marcia. Oh that's right, she's not in the office now. (*To intercom*) Never mind. Well, I'll have to rely on memory.

BOB: Dirigible?

CHARLOTTE: I'm sorry, did I say dirigible? Now what word did I want?

BOB: Blimp?

CHARLOTTE: (*Not understanding*) Blimp?

BOB: Is the word blimp?

CHARLOTTE: (*Irritated*) No it's nothing like blimp. Now you've made me forget what I was saying. (*Holds her head*) Something about apartments. Oh yes. Did you want to meet my son as a possible roommate?

BOB: I don't understand what you're talking about. Why do you want me to meet your son? Is he gay?

CHARLOTTE: (*Offended*) No he's not gay. What an awful thing to suggest. He just wants to share an apartment with someone. Isn't that what you want?

BOB: No it isn't. I have not come to you for real estate advice. I've come to you because my lover and I are in danger of breaking up.

CHARLOTTE: Lover?

BOB: Your patient, Bruce! The person who was just here. He and I are lovers, don't you know that?

CHARLOTTE: Good God, no!

BOB: What do you mean, Good God no!

CHARLOTTE: But he doesn't seem homosexual. He doesn't lisp.

BOB: Are you kidding?

CHARLOTTE: Well, he doesn't lisp, does he? Now what was I thinking of? Be quiet for a moment. (*Holds her head*) Secretary. The word I was looking for was secretary.

BOB: I mean didn't Bruce talk about us? Am I that unimportant to him?

CHARLOTTE: I really can't remember without access to the files. Let's talk about something else.

BOB: Something else?

CHARLOTTE: Oh, tell me about your childhood. At what age did you masturbate?

BOB: I don't want to talk about my childhood.

CHARLOTTE: Very well. We'll just sit in silence. (She *hugs Snoopy*) New patients are difficult, aren't they, Snoopy?

BOB: May I see your accreditation, please?
(Charlotte *starts to empty drawer again*)

BOB: Never mind.

CHARLOTTE: So you and Bruce are an item, eh? Odd, that I didn't pick that up.

BOB: Well we may be an item no longer.

75

CHARLOTTE: Well the path of true love never doth run smoothly.

BOB: I mean, suddenly there are all these women.

CHARLOTTE: Well if you're homosexual, I guess you don't find me attractive then, do you?

BOB: What?

CHARLOTTE: I guess you don't find me attractive, do you?

BOB: I don't see what that has to do with anything.

CHARLOTTE: Very well. We'll drop the subject. (*Pause*) Not even a teensy weensy bit? Well, no matter. (*Pause*) Tell me. What do you and Bruce do exactly?

BOB: What do you mean?

CHARLOTTE: You know what I mean. Physically.

BOB: I don't care to discuss it.

CHARLOTTE: Tell me.

BOB: Why do you want to know?

CHARLOTTE: Patients act out many of their deepest conflicts through the sexual act. Women who get on top may wish to feel dominant. Men who prefer oral sex with women may wish to return to the womb. Couples who prefer the missionary position may wish to do anthropological work in Ghana. Everything people do is a clue to a trained psychotherapist. (*Pause*) Tell me! Tell me!

BOB: I don't care to talk about it.

CHARLOTTE: Very well. We'll move on to something else. (*Sulks*) I'm sure I can guess what goes on anyway. (*Sulks*) I wasn't born yesterday. (*Pause; screams*) COCK-SUCKER!

BOB: What?

CHARLOTTE: Oh, I'm sorry. It was just a terrible urge I had. I'm terribly sorry. (*Gleefully*) COCKSUCKER! (*Screams with laughter, clutches Snoopy, rocks back and forth*) Oh my goodness, I'm sorry, I'm sorry. COCKSUCKER! Whoops! Sorry. Oh God, it's my blood sugar. Help, I need a cookie. Help, a cookie! COCKSUCKER! Wait, don't leave, I think I have a cookie in one of the drawers. Oh, I'm going to say it again, oh God! (*Covers her mouth, screams the word into her hand, it's muffled. Slams drawers open and closed, finds a bag of chocolate chip cookies, rams several into her mouth*) Mmmm, cookie, cookie. Oh God. (*Collapses, lets arms dangle, leans back in chair*) Oh God. (*Laughs lightly*) Oh, that was wonderful.

BOB: (*Stands, takes out a gun*) It's people like you who've oppressed gay people for centuries. (*Shoots her several times*)

CHARLOTTE: (*Startled; then*) Good for you! Bravo! I like that. You're expressing your feelings, people have got to express their feelings. Am I bleeding? I can't find any blood.

BOB: It's a starting pistol. I bought it a couple of days ago, to threaten Bruce with.

CHARLOTTE: Good for you!

BOB: I don't want to go to prison. That's the only reason it's not a real gun.

CHARLOTTE: Good reason. You know what you want, and what you don't want. Oh I like this directness, I feel I'm starting to help you. I mean, don't you see the similarity? Now why don't I have ulcers? Do you know?

BOB: I don't know what you're talking about.

CHARLOTTE: I don't have ulcers because I don't repress things. I admit to all my feelings. Now a few minutes ago when I wanted to hurl anti-homosexual epithets at you, I didn't repress myself, I just let 'em rip. And that's why I'm happy. And when you were mad at me, you took out your toy gun and you shot me. And that's the beginning of mental health. I mean, do you understand what I'm saying?

BOB: Well I follow you.

CHARLOTTE: Oh we're making progress. Don't you see? And you said it yourself. You didn't buy the gun to shoot me, you bought it to shoot Bruce and that floozie of his. Right?

BOB: Yes.

CHARLOTTE: So you see what I'm getting at?

BOB: You mean, I should follow through on my impulse and go shoot Bruce and Prudence?

CHARLOTTE: Oh I've never had such a productive first session!

BOB: But should I get a real gun, or just use this one?

CHARLOTTE: That would be up to you. You have to ask yourself what you *really* want.

BOB: Well I don't want to go to jail. I just want to punish them.

CHARLOTTE: Good! Punish them! Act it out!

BOB: I mean, I could go to that restaurant right now.

CHARLOTTE: Oh yes! Oh good!

BOB: Will you come with me? I mean, in case someone tries to stop me you can explain it's part of my therapy.

CHARLOTTE: Okay, let me just have another cookie. Oh, I'm so glad you came to me. Now, should I bring Snoopy with me, or leave him here?

BOB: Well, what do you really *want*?

CHARLOTTE: Oh you're right. That's the issue—good for you. Okay, now . . . I don't know which I want. Let me sit here for a moment and figure it out.
(She *sits and thinks, weighing pro-and-con-Snoopy ideas in her head; lights dim*).

ACT II

Scene 2

The restaurant. Prudence *and* Bruce.

BRUCE: Prudence . . . will you marry me?

PRUDENCE: Why have we come back to this restaurant? We've been here twice before and never got any service.

BRUCE: I'm sentimental about it. It's where we first met. You're ignoring my proposal.

PRUDENCE: Bruce, really. You can't be serious. I mean, your friend Bob carries on like Camille . . .

BRUCE: But Bob isn't the issue. We are. I mean, I'm really fond of Bob, I guess I love him—there, I've said it—but he'll learn to accept us. I mean, I need the stability of a woman. I want children. Bob will visit. The children will love him. He and I can go on weekend hunting trips from time to time.

81

PRUDENCE: Well, that all sounds wonderful and tempting indeed. Bob's mother and I will learn to perform selections from "Flower Drum Song." But all that aside, I mean isn't this all rather hilariously premature?

BRUCE: Prudence, I believe one should act—without thought, without reason, act on instinct. Look at the natives in Samoa, look at Margaret Mead. Did they think about what they were doing?

PRUDENCE: But . . .

BRUCE: I have this instinct that we'd be right together. Why don't we make a leap of faith, like Nietzsche or Kierkegaard said, just *leap* into it. What's the worst that can happen? We'll have made a mistake, we'll get a no-fault divorce, we'll be none the worse for it. We'll be *wiser*. And the other option is that we might discover incredible happiness together.

PRUDENCE: I don't understand you. We've known each other a week.

BRUCE: A week can be an eternity.

PRUDENCE: Yes, and if it rains, it's even worse. God, I wish you wouldn't say pretentious things.

BRUCE: You're right, that was pretentious. But my point is that sometimes a week is enough to get to know someone. And marriage should be about discovery too. It's good not to know everything.

PRUDENCE: I just don't know how to explain to you how silly an idea it is.

BRUCE: I mean, don't you want to get married sometime? Aren't you afraid of being lonely?

PRUDENCE: Well, I suppose I am.

BRUCE: And aren't all your girlfriends from college married by now?

PRUDENCE: Well certainly many of them are.

BRUCE: And your sister's married. Your *younger* sister.

PRUDENCE: Well it's not a contest.

BRUCE: And you know you should really have children now, particularly if you may want more than one. I mean, soon you'll be at the end of your child-bearing years. I don't mean to be mean bringing that up; but it is a reality.

PRUDENCE: Well that's true, it *is* a consideration. And I really do think I want to have children. But . . . (She's *starting to get upset*)

BRUCE: I mean, time is running out for you. And me too. I mean we're not twenty anymore. We're not even twenty-six anymore. Do you remember how old thirty used to seem?

PRUDENCE: Please don't go on, you're making me hysterical.

BRUCE: No, but these are realities, Prudence. I may be your last chance, maybe no one else will want to marry you until you're forty. And it's hard to meet people. You already said that Shaun Cassidy was too young. I mean, we have so little time left to ourselves, we've got to grab it before it's gone.
(Stuart *enters, sees them, hides behind a table*)

PRUDENCE: Oh stop talking about time please. I mean, I know I'm thirty, it doesn't mean I'm dead.

BRUCE: I didn't say dead. I just said that our time on this earth is limited.

PRUDENCE: Stop talking, stop talking. (*Covers her ears*)

BRUCE: Prudence, I think you and I can make each other happy. (*Looks behind her*) Do you see someone over there? Is that a waiter *hiding*?

PRUDENCE: Oh for God's sake.

BRUCE: What is it?

PRUDENCE: It's my therapist.

BRUCE: Here?

PRUDENCE: I thought we were being followed. (*Calling*) Dr. Framingham, we see you.

BRUCE: What's he doing here?
(Stuart *comes over to them*)

STUART: I want you to leave here with me this instant.

PRUDENCE: Why are you following me?

STUART: I'm going to give you a prescription for a sedative, and then I'm going to drive you home.

PRUDENCE: I can't believe that you've been following me.

STUART: I care about my patients. (*To Bruce*) She's really *very* sick. The work we have to do together will take years.

PRUDENCE: Dr. Framingham, I've been meaning to call you since our last session. I'm discontinuing my therapy with you.

STUART: That would be very self-destructive. You'd be in Bellevue in a week.

PRUDENCE: I really don't want to see you ever again. Please go away now.

STUART: (*To* Bruce) She wants to stop therapy. I can't believe how self-destructive that is. The poor woman is going through a self-identity problem which is very serious.

PRUDENCE: Self-identity is redundant.

STUART: It's the content that matters, not how it's said.

PRUDENCE: Then listen to this content please: leave the restaurant. Go away.

STUART: You don't mean what you say.

BRUCE: Do you want me to hit him?

PRUDENCE: No, I just want him to go away.

BRUCE: The lady wants you to leave, mister.

STUART: (*To* Prudence) So this is the degenerate you told me about?

BRUCE: What did she tell you about me?

PRUDENCE: Bruce, don't talk to him, please. Stuart, leave the restaurant. I'm tired of this.

STUART: Not until we set up our next appointment.

PRUDENCE: But, Stuart, I *told* you I'm discontinuing our therapy.

STUART: You haven't explained why to me.

PRUDENCE: Then I will. BECAUSE YOU ARE A PREMA-TURE EJACULATOR AND A LOUSY THERAPIST. NOW BEAT IT!

STUART: (*Very hurt, very mad*)
Okay, Miss Sensuous woman. But do you know what's going to happen to you without therapy? You're going to become a very pathetic, very lonely old maid.
(*To Bruce*)
She has very serious problems relating to men and to sex; she belittles men because she's so insecure herself. I mean, she is really frightened!
(*Back to Prudence*)
I mean, you know what's going to happen to you? You're going to break off with this clown in a few days, and then you're not going to go out with men anymore at all, and you'll tell yourself it's because there aren't any men good enough for you, but it's because you're so afraid somebody's gonna see through you that you're so tough on everybody else. Your emotional life is going to be tied up with your cats!
(*To Bruce*)
Do you know what she does in her apartment? She keeps cats! Some guy she almost married last year wanted to marry her but he was allergic to cats, and so *she* chose the cats!

PRUDENCE: That's not why we broke up at all!

STUART: You're gonna end up taking little boat cruises to Bermuda with your cats and with spinster librarians when you're fifty unless you decide to kill yourself before then! And all because you were too cowardly and self-destructive and stupid to keep yourself from being an old maid by sticking with your therapy!

86

PRUDENCE: You are talking utter gibberish. Michael was only *slightly* allergic to cats, and we didn't get married because we decided we weren't really in love. And there's nothing wrong with keeping cats. And I will never go on a cruise to Bermuda. I hate Bermuda! And I'm not going to end up an old maid, I'm going to get married and have at least two children; in fact, I may even marry Bruce here. And if I do, Bruce and I will send you a picture of our children every Christmas to the mental institution where you'll be locked up!

STUART: (*Hysterical*) You're a terrible, terrible patient!

PRUDENCE: And you're a hideous doctor! I hate you!
(They *throw water at each other. Enter* Bob *and* Mrs. Wallace)

CHARLOTTE: Hello, everybody!

STUART: Who are these people?

CHARLOTTE: Go ahead, Bob, tell them.

BOB: I want to tell you how you've made me feel. I feel very angry.
(He *takes out his gun;* Prudence, Bruce *and* Stuart *look terrified. He fires the gun at them six or seven times. They are terribly shocked, stunned; are trying to figure out if they've been hit and are dying.
Enter a young* Waiter)

WAITER: I'm sorry. We're going to have to ask you people to leave.

BRUCE: But we haven't even seen menus.

WAITER: I'm sorry. We can't have shootings in here.

STUART: Oh my God. Oh my God.
(*Feels himself all over for wounds, just coming out of his fear*)

PRUDENCE: (*Taking the gun from* Bob) Give me that. (*Points the gun at the* Waiter) Now look here, you. I am sick of the service in this restaurant. *I am very hungry.* Now I want you to bring me a steak, medium rare, no potato, two vegetables, a small salad with oil and vinegar, and a glass of red wine. (*Angry, grouchy*) Anyone else want to order?

CHARLOTTE: I'd like to see a menu.

PRUDENCE: (*Waving the gun*) And bring these other people menus. And make it snappy.

WAITER: Yes, ma'am. (*Exits in a hurry*)

CHARLOTTE: (*To Prudence) Oh I *like* your directness. Bravo!

STUART: (*Feeling for bullet holes*) I don't understand. Did he miss all of us?

PRUDENCE: Shut up and sit down. I'm going to eat some dinner, and I want everyone to shut up.

CHARLOTTE: Oh, I think she's marvelous.

PRUDENCE: (*Aims the gun at her*) Shut up.

CHARLOTTE: Sorry.
(*Everyone sits quietly. Waiter brings menus, which people look at, except for* Prudence, *who glares and* Stuart *who's shaken*)

WAITER: Our specials today are chicken marsala, cooked in a garlic and white wine sauce . . .
(*Lights dim to black*)

88

ACT II

Scene 3

The restaurant still. They've finished their dinners: Prudence, Bruce, Bob, Mrs. Wallace, Stuart. The Waiter is clearing the dishes.

CHARLOTTE: Mmmmm, that chocolate mousse was delicious. I really shouldn't have had two.

WAITER: (*To* Prudence) Will there be anything else?

PRUDENCE: Just the check please.

STUART: (*Who's still in a sort of shock; to* Bob) I thought you'd killed us all. You should be locked up.

BOB: Well, all's well that ends well.

CHARLOTTE: Please, I thought we'd exhausted the whole topic of the shooting. No harm was done.

STUART: What if I'd had a heart condition?

CHARLOTTE: That would have been your responsibility. We must all take responsibility for our own lives.

STUART: I think you're a terrible therapist.

CHARLOTTE: Sounds like professional jealousy to me.

PRUDENCE: (*To* Stuart) I would not bring up the subject of who's a terrible therapist if I were you.

CHARLOTTE: (*To* Bruce) She's so direct. I just find her wonderful. Congratulations, Bruce.

PRUDENCE: What are you congratulating him on?

CHARLOTTE: Aren't you getting married?

BRUCE: Yes.   PRUDENCE: No.
(*Re-enter* Waiter *with the check*)

WAITER: Here's the check. The second chocolate mousse was on the house, Mrs. Wallace.

CHARLOTTE: Thank you, honey. (*Kisses him on the cheek;* Waiter *exits*)

CHARLOTTE: He's one of my patients too.

BOB: He's quite attractive.

BRUCE: I thought you were going to kill yourself.

BOB: Mrs. Wallace helped me express my anger, and now I don't feel like it anymore.

STUART: If one runs around shooting off guns, blank or otherwise, just because one is angry, then we'll have anarchy.

BOB: No one is interested in your opinion.

BRUCE: I think Prudence and I are a good match. I think we should get married as soon as possible.

PRUDENCE: I never want to get married, ever. I'm going to quit my job, and stay in my apartment until they evict me. Then I'm going to become a bag lady and live in the tunnels under Grand Central Station.

(They all *stare at her*)

BRUCE: (*To* Prudence) If you marry me, I'll help you want to live again.

BOB: What am I supposed to do?

BRUCE: You seemed too busy with the waiter a minute ago.

BOB: For God's sake, I just looked at him. You're trying to go off and marry this woman. Really, you're just impossible. I thought after I shot at you, you'd get over this silly thing about women.

BRUCE: I need the stability of a woman.

BOB: You think she's stable? She just said she was going to become a bag woman.

BRUCE: She was speaking metaphorically.

BOB: What kind of metaphor is becoming a bag woman?

BRUCE: She meant she was depressed.

BOB: So I'm depressed too. Why don't you marry me? We'll go find some crackpot Episcopal minister somewhere, and then we'll adopt children together.

BRUCE: And that's another thing. I want to have my own children. I want to reproduce. She can give me children.

PRUDENCE: Please stop talking about me that way. I don't want to have your children. I want to be left alone. I want to take a cruise to Bermuda with spinster librarians. I want to become a lesbian and move in with Kate Millett.

BOB: Now she's making sense.

BRUCE: Don't make fun of her. She's upset.

BOB: I'm upset. No one worries about me.

BRUCE: Prudence, don't cry. We'll live in Connecticut. Everything will be fine.

PRUDENCE: (*Exasperated, but trying to be kind for a moment*) Bruce, you're not the right person for me. When I find the right person I'll marry him.

BRUCE: Mrs. Wallace, say something to her.

CHARLOTTE: Prudence, there is no right person. Don't you agree, Dr. Framingham? Everyone in this world is limited; and depending on one's perspective is either horrible or okay. Isn't that so, Dr. Framingham?

STUART: I'll have to think about it.

CHARLOTTE: Prudence, stop running away from facts. Face it, we're all alone, everyone's crazy, and you have no choice but to be alone or to be with someone in what will be a highly imperfect and probably eventually unsatisfactory relationship.

PRUDENCE: I don't believe that's true.

CHARLOTTE: But you do. That's exactly why you act the way you do, because you believe that.

PRUDENCE: I believe there's more chance for happiness than that.

CHARLOTTE: You don't! And why should you? Look at Chekhov. Masha loves Konstantin, but Konstantin only loves Nina. Nina doesn't love Konstantin, but falls in love with Trigorin. Trigorin doesn't love Nina but sort of loves Madame Arkadina, who doesn't love anyone but herself. And Medviedenko loves Masha, but she only loves Konstantin, which is where we started out. And then at the end of the play, Konstantin kills himself. Don't you see?

PRUDENCE: I find what you've just said very depressing.

BOB: So do I.

BRUCE: But you haven't understood. Mrs. Wallace just means that because the world is imperfect, Prudence mustn't expect to find perfection. And thus marriage to me wouldn't be so bad.

STUART: Why doesn't she marry me? I make a good living. Prudence, as your therapist, I think you should marry me.

BRUCE: Prudence would never marry a man who didn't cry.

STUART: What?

BRUCE: You're too macho. Prudence doesn't want to marry you.

STUART: There's no such thing as macho. There's male and female, and then there's whatever you are.
(Bruce *cries*)

STUART: Oh, I'm sorry. Was it what I said?

93

CHARLOTTE: Bruce cries all the time. I encourage him to.

BRUCE: (*Having stopped crying; to* Prudence) Why won't you marry me?

STUART: She should marry me.

PRUDENCE: No. I don't want to marry either of you. You're both crazy. I'm going to marry someone sane.

BOB: There's just me left.

PRUDENCE: No. I'll marry the waiter. Waiter!

CHARLOTTE: Oh dear, poor thing. Fear of intimacy leading to faulty reality testing. Prudence, dear, you don't know the waiter.

PRUDENCE: That doesn't matter. Bruce said it's better to know nothing about people when you get married.

BRUCE: But I meant you should marry me.

PRUDENCE: But I know too much about you and I know nothing about the waiter. Waiter!
(*Enter* Waiter)

WAITER: Is something the matter?

PRUDENCE: Yes. I want you to marry me.

WAITER: I don't understand. Did I add the check wrong?

PRUDENCE: No. I want you to marry me. I only have a few more years in which it's safe to have children.

WAITER: I don't understand.

94

CHARLOTTE: It's all right, Andrew. She's in therapy with me now.

PRUDENCE: (*Takes the blank gun. Aims it at him*) Marry me! Marry me! (*Starts to giggle*) Marry me!

CHARLOTTE: It's all right, Prudence; you're my patient now. Everything's going to be all right.

PRUDENCE: I don't want any more therapy! I want tennis lessons!

CHARLOTTE: Now, dear, you're not ready for tennis yet. You must let me help you.

STUART: She's my patient.

CHARLOTTE: I think you've already failed her. I think I shall have to take her on.

PRUDENCE: (*Screams*) I don't want either of you! I don't want any more therapy! I've been to see several therapists, and I'm sick of talking about myself! (*Suddenly exhausted*) I have to go home and go to sleep. I want to forget meeting all of you.

BRUCE: I'll take you home, Prudence.

PRUDENCE: I'll see myself home, thank you.

BRUCE: Well, I'll call you tomorrow.

PRUDENCE: Please do not call me tomorrow.

BRUCE: But I don't understand.

PRUDENCE: I suggest you put another ad in the paper. (*Hands Bob the gun*) I believe this is yours. Good night. (*Exits*)

CHARLOTTE: Well she's very lovely, but emotionally so blocked.

STUART: I know. We've been working on it, but she fights me so hard.

CHARLOTTE: Well you see she needs a woman therapist who can empathize with her. I mean, I think you're much too much of a masculine figure to be her therapist.

STUART: Do you think I seem masculine?

CHARLOTTE: Oh yes. Very much so.

BOB: (*To* Waiter) Hi, my name is Bob. We haven't actually met yet.

WAITER: Oh, hi.
(He's *clearing dishes, presumably*)

STUART: You know, I think I intimidate many of my women patients by seeming so masculine.

CHARLOTTE: You must learn to discover the feminine part of yourself.

BOB: (*To* Waiter) Would you care to join us for coffee?

WAITER: Thanks. I have other tables to see to.

BOB: Well another time.
(Waiter *exits*)

BOB: (*Said genuinely*) I hate being attracted to people. It's exhausting.

BRUCE: Mrs. Wallace, she seems very angry with me.

CHARLOTTE: Who, dear?

BRUCE: Prudence.

CHARLOTTE: Oh well, she's a very angry person, I saw that right away. Uh, I'm getting a rush from all that mousse. Anyone feel like going to a disco?

BRUCE: Not particularly.

STUART: (*To* Charlotte) You know, all my patients break off their therapy. It's very upsetting.

CHARLOTTE: Would you like to talk about it?
(*Enter* Andrew *the waiter*)

ANDREW: (*To* Bob, *handing him a drink*) I thought you might like a drink. It's on the house.

BOB: Oh thank you.

ANDREW: I get off in five minutes.

BOB: (*Bit of a leer*) Need any help?
(Andrew *grins. The* others *look utterly appalled and stare at* Bob. Andrew *exits;* Bob *says to the* others)

BOB: Sorry.

BRUCE: What are you doing?

BOB: Well if you're allowed to go off with women whenever you feel like it, then I'm allowed to go off with an occasional waiter.

BRUCE: Well I suppose that's fair. It just doesn't feel fair.

BOB: Well it is.

CHARLOTTE: Why is everybody so grumpy? Let's go to a disco!

STUART: I've never been to a disco.

CHARLOTTE: Then you must come. Bob and Bruce?

BOB: I'm game.

BRUCE: Your mood has certainly lightened.

BOB: Venting hostility makes one feel better.

BRUCE: I don't want to go. You all go.

CHARLOTTE: Oh come. It'll be good for you.

BRUCE: I do not feel like going to a disco.

CHARLOTTE: Oh, he's being sulky.

BRUCE: I mean, nothing's gone particularly right. I don't see why I should feel like dancing.

BOB: All right. I won't go if you don't want to.

BRUCE: No, go ahead. I really don't care what you do. Maybe the waiter will want to go.

CHARLOTTE: Oh, Andrew is an excellent dancer! (*To* Bob) His name is Andrew, and he dances very well. He's been to reform school. (*Calls*) Andrew! We're going dancing. (Andrew *enters*)

BRUCE: I'm going to try Prudence. (*To* Andrew) Do you have a pay phone here?

ANDREW: (*Points Off Left*) Yeah, it's over there.

BOB: Bruce, do you want us to wait for you? I mean, I don't have to go dancing if you don't want me to.

BRUCE: No, I'd rather you didn't wait. (*Softer*) Go ahead dancing, it's okay. I need some time to sulk. Good night. (*Goes Off to phone*)

BOB: Oh dear. He's angry.

CHARLOTTE: Oh who cares? Let's go dancing!

BOB: I wonder if he's going to cry.

STUART: He certainly cries a lot.

CHARLOTTE: Don't you ever cry, Dr. Framingham?

STUART: Only when things fall on me.

CHARLOTTE: Oh yes. Do you all remember Skylab? That upset my porpoises very much.

STUART: You have porpoises?

CHARLOTTE: I'm sorry, did I say porpoises? Andrew, what word do I want?

ANDREW: Patients.

CHARLOTTE: Yes, thank you. Patients.

ANDREW: We had this guy in reform school that we didn't like much. So we took this big heavy metal bird bath, and we dropped it on him. He didn't cry.

CHARLOTTE: That's interesting, Andrew.

ANDREW: He went into a coma.

CHARLOTTE: (*Stern*) Andrew, I've told you, I want you to have *empathy* for people.

ANDREW: Oh right. I forgot. (*To Bob and Stuart*) We felt real bad for him.

CHARLOTTE: Andrew has a real sensitivity in him that we just haven't discovered yet.

BOB: How long were you in reform school?

ANDREW: About three years. (*With a grin*) Till it burned down.

BOB: (*To Charlotte*) Maybe I should wait around for Bruce.

CHARLOTTE: Oh nonsense. He needs time to be by himself. The music is calling us.

BOB: Well all right.

ANDREW: (*Pointing out to Up Left*) My motorcycle's out this way.

BOB: My mother doesn't like me to ride motorcycles.

ANDREW: (*Shrugged off*) Fuck her.

STUART: (*To Charlotte*) I don't think I want to go. I don't like crowds.

CHARLOTTE: Don't be silly.

STUART: There'll be too many women. I shouldn't tell you this, but I have troubles relating to women.

CHARLOTTE: Not to me. I think you're delightful.

STUART: You do?

CHARLOTTE: You know what I think? I think I could help you. I think you should come into therapy with me. I don't mean therapy, I mean thermidor.

ANDREW: No, you mean therapy.

CHARLOTTE: Do I? It doesn't sound right. Thermidor. Thorazine. Thermometer.

BOB: No, he's right, you mean therapy.

CHARLOTTE: Therapy. Therapy? Thackery. Thespian. The Second Mrs. Tanqueray. Ftatateeta. Uh, well, whatever.
(All four *start to exit out Up Left*)

CHARLOTTE: (*To Stuart*) You know, there's a very interesting play called *Equus* in which the main character, Dr. Dysart, with whom I greatly identify . . .
(*They're out. After a moment* Prudence *enters from Up Right. She looks around confused, surprised to see no one there. Enter* Bruce *from Down Left*)

BRUCE: Oh. I was just calling you.

PRUDENCE: Oh. Well I'm not home.

BRUCE: Yes.

PRUDENCE: Where is everybody?

BRUCE: They went to a disco.

PRUDENCE: I don't understand. Everybody was fighting, and then they went to a disco?

BRUCE: Mrs. Wallace said it had something to do with the mousse she ate.

PRUDENCE: Never mind, I don't want to know. I only came back because I didn't pay for my meal.

BRUCE: Oh, well. I think Mrs. Wallace took you, me and Bob as a business deduction.

PRUDENCE: Well I don't want her to do that. (*Holds out money*) Would you give her this for me please?

BRUCE: Really, she won't accept it. I think she enjoyed the evening.

PRUDENCE: Well I'll mail it to her. I don't like being in anyone's debt.

BRUCE: You can't go through life never being in anyone's debt.

PRUDENCE: I can try. What's her address?

BRUCE: Why did you really come back to the restaurant?

PRUDENCE: I don't know. I went for a walk. And then I didn't feel like being angry with you anymore.

BRUCE: I'm really glad if you're not so mad anymore. I was calling you up to apologize. I mean, Sally hates me. It would be horrible to think of you hating me too.

PRUDENCE: Well I don't hate you. I think Bob may, if you're not careful.

BRUCE: I'm really not running my life very well right now. You see, I like you both so much, I wanted you to like each other too.

PRUDENCE: Well, all's well that ends well, ha ha ha.

BRUCE: Yes.

PRUDENCE: Do you think Mrs. Wallace is right? That people are either horrible or okay?

BRUCE: Oh, therapists say a lot of things just to get a reaction. I don't think she means it.

PRUDENCE: I think she does mean it. Doesn't seem to bother her much though.

BRUCE: If you had to categorize me one way or another, would you consider me horrible or okay?

PRUDENCE: (*Smiles*) I would consider you "okay."

BRUCE: (*Pleased*) Thank you. You know, when I was phoning you, I realized why I feel so emotionally drawn to you. You see, all my life I keep fluctuating between being traditional and being insane. Like Sally and the brain scan and the Book of Leviticus were my trying to be traditional; while sleeping with the gas man or that time I took my clothes off in the dentist's office were my going to the opposite extreme. But I'm not happy at either extreme. And that's where you fit in. I mean, I think you're very traditional, like Sally, and I like that about both of you, but Sally had no flexibility or imagination, she was too stable. But I think that even though you're traditional, that you're very *un*stable, and because of that I think we could be very happy together. Do you understand what I'm saying?

PRUDENCE: (*Not being flip*) I don't understand what happened at the dentist's office.

BRUCE: (*A bit offended*) It doesn't matter what happened at the dentist's office. The point is . . . well, the point is I thought you liked me.

PRUDENCE: (*Soft, a tender rejection*) I do like you. That's why I came back. I think you're . . . fun, and you're very lively, but . . . I don't think we're compatible. I'd be very irritated about the gas man; and I like far fewer emotional peaks and valleys than I think you normally experience.

BRUCE: But people change, Prudence. Just because I slept with the gas man once doesn't mean I'd do it again. And not everyone who comes to read the gas meter is attractive anyway. I mean, I could change. I could try to have fewer peaks and valleys in my life. Mrs. Wallace could put me on lithium.

PRUDENCE: (*Amused, friendly*) Well that's a good idea. She can give me speed, and we'll meet somewhere in the middle.

BRUCE: That's what I mean. Meet in the middle.

PRUDENCE: I just don't feel it would be realistic for us to keep on trying. I don't think I believe that people can change. Or change much anyway.

BRUCE: Oh. Well. I see.

PRUDENCE: I wish I felt otherwise. I really do.

BRUCE: Well I guess you know your own mind.

PRUDENCE: Yes. Well, it was nice to meet you.

BRUCE: It was nice to meet you.
(They *shake hands*. She *kisses his cheek*. They *part*. She *starts to leave, but doesn't go far before she sits down at the table. He sits down too*)

PRUDENCE: I don't feel like going home yet.

BRUCE: Me neither. Maybe we could order an after-dinner drink. The waiter we had has gone off with Bob to the disco, but maybe there's another one.

PRUDENCE: Yes, a drink might be nice.

BRUCE:
(*Calls*)
Oh, waiter. Waiter!

PRUDENCE: (*Calls also*) Waiter! I don't see anybody, do you?

BRUCE: No. Waiter!

PRUDENCE: Waiter!

BRUCE: Waiter. Waiter. This is a very existential restaurant.

PRUDENCE: Yes it is. Waiter. Oh well. It's sort of restful sitting here calling "Waiter."

BRUCE: Yes, I'm quite fond of it. Waiter.

PRUDENCE: Waiter.

BRUCE: (*Sings, making a joke*) There's a waiter that I'm longing dum dum, (*Starts to stare Off and sing the song for real*) Dum dum dum dum . . .
(Prudence *joins* Bruce, *staring Off and singing*)

BRUCE AND PRUDENCE: Dum dum dum dum,
Dum dum dum dum over me . . .

BRUCE: Silly song.

PRUDENCE: Very silly.
(They *stare out, dreamily*)

END